The Engaging EXPERT

a Fieldbook for Occasional Presenters & Accidental Trainers

Terri Cheney
With Sheila Krejci, M Ed HRD

© Copyright 2012 Terri Cheney and Sheila Krejci
All rights reserved.
ISBN: 0985048107
ISBN-13: 9780985048105

DEDICATION

Thanks to many incredible participants, colleagues and clients who continually encourage us to share our insights, ideas and experiences in print, workshops, keynotes and other learning and professional development events.

Special thanks to Tony, Michael and David who continually challenge me to learn and grow in wisdom and patience on this lifelong learning journey.

CONTENTS

Why You Bought This Fieldbook	i
1. Begin with The End in Mind	1
2. Create Rehearsal Opportunities	35
3. Prepare to Engage	81
4. Support Your Message	127
5. WOW Your Audience!	145
6. Measure Your Impact	183
7. What Will *You* DO?	205

WHY YOU BOUGHT THIS FIELDBOOK

Congratulations! Enough people have recognized your expertise in your field that you are being called upon to share what you know with others.

Teaching other people is probably not your primary job, of course. Most of your time is taken up with your "real" work in your area of expertise. You may enjoy delivering occasional presentations and training sessions, or you may find them daunting.

Either way, you have neither the time nor the intent to become a professional speaker or trainer right now, thank you very much. You just want a resource that will help you share what you know more effectively – and ideally in a manner that you enjoy.

One critical thing distinguishes you from others in your position, however.

Most people begin planning their presentations with the question, "What do I want them to *know*?" You, on the other hand, have taken a significant leap by changing one simple word in your question:

"What do I want them to do?"

It may seem like a small difference, but the impact can be profound.

It can reverse the way you plan your presentations. It can slash the amount of lecturing you do. (Your audiences will appreciate that one!) It can mean the difference between a massive "data dump" that has little impact on how your participants do their jobs and a focused transfer of knowledge that their colleagues will notice when your participants return to their usual work.

All from that little shift in your starting question.

This Fieldbook is intended to expedite your efforts in all the key phases of sharing what you know in such a way that other peoples' performance will be noticeably improved.

HOW THIS FIELDBOOK IS ORGANIZED

Since your intent is to affect the way your audience performs back in the Real World rather than simply write a better lecture, this fieldbook walks you through all they key phases of accomplishing that.

1. **Begin with the End in Mind** helps you work backward from identifying the results you want from your presentation or training session back in the Real World of your audience, including figuring out a realistic way to measure the success of your efforts.

2. **Create Rehearsal Opportunities** explains why words are not enough to get your expertise out of your head, and it helps you plan ways for your learners to practice the specific behaviors you want from them after your session. In the Real World hardly anybody is called upon to pass a multiple-choice quiz or to phrase their responses in the form of a question; the Real World is messier and full of demands to make decisions and adapt to changing circumstances. And yes, you can mimic those contexts in a classroom or lecture setting.

3. **Prepare to Engage** gives you dozens of alternatives to lecture for delivering your content and suggests a simple, flexible structure for organizing it.

4. **Support Your Message** helps you transform your PowerPoint and other visual aids into potent tools for helping your participants learn, and it suggests tips for making effective handouts and job aids.

5. **Wow Your Audience!** covers high-impact techniques that will add polish to your actual delivery. It should make your time in front of a group considerably easier and, we hope, more enjoyable for all parties concerned.

6. **Measure Your Impact** loops back to the measures of success you identified at the start of the project, helping you demonstrate the value of what you delivered.

Lots of Examples

Every chapter is loaded with examples. All of them are derived from the Real World experience of Terri and Sheila and, in some cases, a few of our colleagues. We removed the names and other identifying information – partly because of our confidentiality agreements with many of our clients, but also to encourage you to fill in our own details from a similar context familiar to you. The more we can help you imagine applying what you learn, the better you are likely to learn it.

Working *With* the Human Brain

Where it is appropriate, we will include bite-sized explanations of *why* we recommend certain techniques over others. We draw on current brain science and adult learning theory to help you make your material stick. We'll keep it in plain language – just like you will opt for plain language in *your* area of expertise when it is helpful for your audience.

A Word About Vocabulary

This fieldbook is intended for a variety of situations, including one-time presentations, workshops of varying lengths, and classes explicitly labeled "training." We will use these terms interchangeably throughout the book.

So you needn't be alarmed if you see the word "training" when your purpose is to prepare a one-time presentation. Nor should you dismay if you see "presentation" when you are working on a workshop or training. Our recommendations will serve you well in all of these contexts, since your objective is to affect what your listeners *do* afterward.

What Will *You* Do?

In that same spirit, what do you anticipate *you* will do differently after digging into this resource? What will it take to make your investment of time and attention to this material pay off? And how will you be able to tell if is has, in fact, been worthwhile?

We invite you to challenge yourself – and challenge this material the way your own audiences might challenge yours. By starting your own learning experience with a measurable end clearly in mind, you are already applying the first principle of this fieldbook. You are already practicing the sort of thing you want to do back in your Real World.

Your shift in your starting question, from "What do I want them to *know*?" to "What do I want them to *do*?" reverses the way most people plan presentations.

This has the paradoxical effect of prolonging the initial time it takes to identify the purpose and target outcomes of your presentation, and shortening the time it takes to put all the pieces together. Your total prep time can remain the same or even shrink. But this still is not a comfortable way of operating for most people in your position.

The next chapter walks you through a methodical way of working backwards from the end results you want in the Real World to selecting the specific content you want to share.

The pay-off is worth it.

BEGIN WITH THE END IN MIND

*"Audiences don't care what you say;
they only care about what they are
left with after you've said it."*

— Andy Bounds, *The Jelly Effect*

Most people, when asked to share their expertise in a one-to-multiple setting like training or a workshop, leap right to sorting through what content they should cover. This is a little bit like starting to paint a room by slapping color on the walls without first covering the furniture or taping around windows and doors to protect the frames.

You can choose to paint a room this way, of course. And you may very well get a perfectly satisfactory result. But even the most inexperienced visitor will notice a dramatic difference compared with a room that was more carefully prepped before the actual painting started.

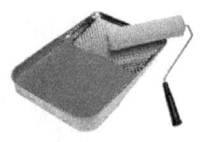A novice painter might lament the up-front time it takes to do all the prep work. Is it really necessary to wash the walls and use such an extravagant number of drop cloths? Why expend so much effort painstakingly covering the baseboards? Using a small brush to paint around outlets and window frames could be skipped if you were just really careful with the paint roller, right?

The veteran knows that taking time at the beginning to prep the room ends up saving time in the end. And when a room is properly prepped, rolling the paint on to large stretches of wall is the fastest, easiest part of the whole job.

So it is with the content of your session. When you take the time to do the presentation equivalent of moving the furniture and so forth, then filling in the details of what information to include becomes the simplest, fastest step in the whole process. And the end result will be something you are happy to show off in the Real World.

So what, exactly, is the "prep work" of creating a workshop? It starts with some penetrating questions, such as:

- ❏ Why is this presentation (or workshop/training/etc.) really necessary in the first place?
- ❏ How does it support IRACIS, goddess of business objectives? (We'll introduce IRACIS shortly.)
- ❏ Is it really a transfer-of-knowledge issue?
- ❏ Who is going to be there?
- ❏ What happens afterward?
- ❏ How will you know it worked?

Taking time to dig into these questions before you start planning your presentation will save you (and probably lots of other folks) plenty of time, money and heartburn later on. It even might make you something of a hero as you not only save participants from a poorly targeted "information dump" but also help the bottom line of the organization.

❏ *Is this presentation (or workshop/training/etc.) really necessary in the first place?*

This may seem like a strange question to use at the start of a book on helping other adults learn. But the query is not flippant. *Will the impact or value of your session be greater than the real cost?* Think about it. In-person workshops are more costly than meets the eye, and the expenses start piling up well before participant supplies and refreshments are ordered. Let's crunch some hypothetical numbers to illustrate the point. Imagine Luis is a shift supervisor in a small manufacturing company. His boss, the vice-president of fulfillment, has asked him to prepare a one-time, three-hour workshop on how to speed up ordering using the new system. The real-cost numbers might look like this:

Luis spends a total of 140 hours on all aspects of the project, including researching and writing the content, getting approvals, and handling the follow-up after the session. He also spends time practicing before delivering the three-hour session. His time costs the company $28 per hour.	$3,920
Luis's boss, the VP of fulfillment and the person who requested the training in the first place, spends a grand total of about an hour on the project: explaining what she needs Luis to provide, and reviewing and giving him feedback on his progress. Her time costs the company $45 per hour.	$45

3

The VP's administrative assistant is tasked with booking the space, ordering refreshments, preparing participant materials, and making sure everything is in place on the day of the training. She spends 32 hours on the project, and her time costs the company $25 per hour.	$800
A total of 38 employees participate in the session. Their time costs the company an average of $22 per hour.	$2,508
Supplies, participant materials and refreshments cost the company a total of $235.	$235
Total Expenditures:	$7,508

Who knew the real cost to the company for a single three-hour workshop would be in the neighborhood of $7,500?!

Just to push the point further, imagine the opportunity cost of the 522 hours invested by all the people affected. If they had not been involved in preparing and participating in the training, what could they have been doing instead that might have generated more revenue for the company? Or reduced costs or improved service?

How about a more constrained example. What if you have been asked to present something as part of a larger meeting? Let's say you are a physician recently back from an administrative summit, and now you will share the latest organization-wide news with staff at your particular site.

Odds are you will spend at least a little bit of time preparing what you are going to say. Let's make it a round number and say you devote an hour total to preparing your remarks and roughing out some PowerPoint slides. Your administrative assistant dedicates another hour to making the actual slides, and preparing and copying handouts. If your time costs the clinic $225 per hour, and your assistant's time is $25 per hour, you have invested a total of $250 so far just to prepare a 30-minute presentation that you haven't even given yet.

Now add in the time of your audience, mostly other physicians, physician assistants and nurse practitioners, with their time costing the clinic an average of $200. Even if you only have 10 people in the room for your half-hour of the larger meeting, that's $1,000 for their time—not to mention another $112.50 for yours. Are you willing to spend resources on that scale for something that may have little if any impact?

So to ask if a live, facilitated session is really necessary in the first place is no trivial question. What makes this training more valuable than the time, expense and resources it will cost to create and deliver it? How will the organization be better off after this workshop than before it? Could you get the same results with a memo or a video?

How would you calculate the cost of your presentation?

Supervisor training for ... non-supervisors

Sheila asked routine discovery questions (like those listed earlier in this chapter) about an eight-hour workshop she had been asked to present on completing the organization's new performance-evaluation forms.

Who was the audience? IT managers.

How many direct reports did most of them have? None.

None? None of the IT managers currently had any direct reports.

Okay, how soon would they start having direct reports under the new structure then? There were no plans to have anyone reporting directly to the IT managers.

The sponsor wanted to proceed with the training anyway. Fortunately Sheila was able to persuade this sponsor to shift the focus of the training to the managers' *own* performance evaluations. Instead of working on providing feedback and guidance for subordinates, participants learned how to write well-crafted goals for themselves and for their short-term project teams of peers, and how to make deliberate use of professional development opportunities to advance their own careers with the company.

POS Training

Sheila was a bit taken aback when she was asking routine discovery questions (like those listed earlier in the chapter) about training she had been asked to prepare for a store's Point-of-Sale (POS) processes.

She was supposed to lead a two-hour *discussion* of the processes.

In a classroom.

With *no* cash registers, credit-card machines, merchandise, customers or currency.

The group was small enough to gather around an unoccupied department register instead, where they practiced several simulations Sheila developed as the primary focus of the training (rather than just discussion). Some participants used the occasion to pick up items they were planning to buy anyway, providing opportunities to complete real transactions.

❑ *How will it support IRACIS, goddess of business objectives?*

To provide real value when you share your expertise with others, you want to make sure the payoff for the organization is greater than all those costs, hidden and otherwise. Usually this means linking your training to IRACIS, the goddess of business objectives.

In principle, every activity in an organization contributes in some way to at least one of three things:

> Increase Revenues
>
> Avoid Costs
>
> Improve Services

You can imagine the acronym for this, IRACIS, this way:

How will your session support IRACIS?

That may look like a throw-away question, but if you cannot connect each part of your training to these outcomes in some way, then, frankly, it probably doesn't belong in your session.

Such an approach to content can seem ruthless at first. Like good prep work for painting a room, however, it ends up making the job easier for everyone involved.

Think your topic is too remote from the front lines to impact IRACIS? Take a closer look. You can almost always connect what you are doing to the larger system. (And if you can't, maybe a presentation is not the best use of the resources involved.)

For example, having all your new hires at a large franchise learn about matching the company's services appropriately to the needs and circumstances of typical customers might at first blush seem like a waste of time for, say, clerical staff. But clerical staff—even those many layers removed from the front line—have a real impact on how customers are served.

> ### *Not Just Any Project-Management Training*
>
> An international perfume company requested project-management training for some of their lead chemists at a research-and-development facility. Project management is a pretty vast subject to say the least. Quite a few probing questions later, it became clear that thousands and sometimes millions of dollars were wasted from poor project-related communication among team leads and sponsors. So Terri linked the project-management training explicitly to the costs of miscommunication among these key stakeholders. This immediately narrowed the focus, making it possible to design crisp rehearsal opportunities that would have a measurable impact on the way the team leads worked.

By positioning your orientation sessions in terms of Increasing Revenues, Avoiding Costs and Improving Service, you help all your employees align their activity with the priorities of the enterprise. The new office manager, for example, can adjust his workflow differently when he can anticipate the needs of staff in the field. The new file clerk, who is the only person to see all the completed work orders, might observe a connection between types of equipment and service problems in the field—and perhaps even gain the franchise an upsell of thousands of dollars.

Here are a few questions to help you start looking for the link between the presentation being asked of you and the business case for it:

❏ Why does management care about this?

❏ How much is this problem really costing, directly and indirectly?

❏ What are your customers concerned about?

❏ What makes this urgent enough to spend company time, money and other resources on it?

Setting: *Manufacturing company requesting customer-service training*

Why does management care about this?

Client satisfaction survey ratings have gone down every year losing business

How much is this problem really costing, directly and indirectly?

We've lost two of our biggest clients this year. Combined sales of over $1.2 million!

What are your customers' saying?

When the Business Journal reported that they were going with XYZ Company, reps were getting questioned about quality.

What makes this urgent enough to spend company time, money and other resources on it at this time?

The new product launch is already behind schedule due to transportation delays; it's imperative that we maintain current customers in order to meet our already strained budget.

> ### Another view: IR-AC-IS?
>
> Author and project-management expert Lou Russell argues that the "IS" in IRACIS is redundant. The net result of a meaningful improvement in service will show up as increased revenue or avoided costs.

❏ Is it really a transfer-of-knowledge issue?

You have heard it before. Someone with decision-making authority says something along the lines of, "They're having trouble keeping up on fourth floor. They need more training on the new system."

Really? Let's take a closer look. What does the person asking for your help mean by "having trouble keeping up"? And what is really causing that issue? Will spending time reviewing the details of the newly installed system solve the problem if what is really slowing down the people on the fourth floor is an unexpected bottleneck created by the new procedures? What if morale on the floor is rock bottom because the supervisor is consistently ineffective? Or maybe a key person is out on maternity leave, and they are short handed.

When you are approached to deliver some sort of expertise-sharing presentation, it pays to do some digging before you start.

Misdiagnosed Call Center

The clinic really and truly did want to improve its service to callers. Patient satisfaction surveys had bottomed out, suggesting that people could not get the help they needed from the triage nurses taking the large volume of calls.

The medical director was livid! They needed new and better protocols. And the staff clearly needed training!

Complex matrices of new protocols and procedures were carefully designed to help the beleaguered triage nurses. Up went a wall chart with daily updates on call wait times so staff would see how much better this new system would be once they were properly trained.

Two weeks into the new protocols, call wait times were *up* over 25 percent!

Not surprisingly, the triage nurses were even more disgruntled than before, when they had been doing their level best to manage the call volume. They had not been consulted on the design of the new protocols they were mandated to use, and they perceived the wall chart as punitive rather than positive.

They got their "see, I told you so" moment. Further investigation revealed that one of the phone lines into the clinic had been severed, and when the phone system was overloaded, incoming calls were immediately lost rather than added to the queue; issues totally unrelated to training or protocols.

Here are a few questions that will help you figure out if training will really address the problem at hand:

❏ What are you hoping to achieve? How can that be measured?

❏ Have participants done this successfully in the past? If yes, what has changed? (e.g. new equipment, new processes, new state mandates, etc.)

❏ What specifically are participants doing now?

❏ What happens if we do nothing?

❏ What are the Real World consequences to individuals if they are not successful? What are the rewards to the individual for outstanding performance? (How do you know people know these?)

❏ Who else is affected by what participants do as a result of this session? Would they be able to tell the difference if someone had or had not participated? How?

How would you adjust these questions to your particular situation?

Setting: *Conflict Management Training for Parks Maintenance Staff*

What are you hoping to achieve? How can that be measured?

Get Parks Department staff to speak respectfully to each other, and handle their own conflicts instead of reporting everything to supervisors. Measures: Less reports to supervisor to intervene; observe respectful language in the workplace.

Have participants done this successfully in the past? If yes, what has changed? (e.g. new equipment, new processes, new state mandates, etc.)

Yes; they're currently always respectful when sponsor is around. Only change is one new supervisor who was promoted from the Recreation Department. In fact, he has reported an inordinate number of complaints coming to his attention for mediation. Sponsor hasn't heard this from other supervisors.

What specifically are they doing now?

Streets maintenance worker complaining that another isn't "pulling his weight" on projects as assigned. Some inappropriate conversation follows. Partner says he hasn't even been notified of the assignments. Two ice arena maintenance workers upset that others left them alone to complete huge project for seasonal opening. Upset with another worker who insists he wasn't assigned to help.

What happens if we do nothing?

The new supervisor will keep coming to sponsor saying, "We need to teach these guys conflict management skills!"

> What are the Real World consequences to individuals if they are not successful? What are the individual's rewards for outstanding performance?
>
> *Supervisor will get fed up and discipline EVERYONE as consequence.*
>
> *Smooth, respectful relations maintained with outstanding performance.*
>
> How do you know people know these?
>
> *Um...not sure they do...*
>
> Who else is affected by what participants do as a result of this session?
>
> Would they be able to tell the difference if someone had not participated? How?
>
> *Me! I'm sick of this. =*
>
> *I should have asked: can you give me examples of how conflict is currently mismanaged. Maybe add note indicating the would-be trainer suspects*
>
> *C/M training is the not right tool?*

What if you discover the biggest factor driving the request for a presentation cannot be addressed effectively with training after all? You generally don't want to say flat-out 'no' to the sponsor making the request. But you do want to suggest options and manage expectations.

What might that look like in the case of the park maintenance staff?

> "So that I can be clear about some of the challenges your supervisors and staff may be facing, I'd like to chat briefly and casually with them. I can do this prior to the start of shifts with everyone so that no one feels singled out."

> "Lots of your people are quite good at customer service. It might be less expensive to provide some coaching for a few people rather than putting everyone through training."

Here are some probing questions you can use in these situations with the sponsor of the presentation or training project.

- ❏ How do others view this situation?
- ❏ What has changed in their environment?
- ❏ What have you tried in the past?
- ❏ Who needs to be involved?
- ❏ Who else is affected by what participants do?
- ❏ What other factors might contribute to that result?
- ❏ How do you currently measure effectiveness?
- ❏ What analysis have you done so far?
- ❏ What will success look like?

What is the first thing you say when someone asks you to share your expertise in the form of a presentation or training?

> "We need you to do a presentation on this topic . . . .
>
> "I'm happy to help you. What is it that your people are not doing or producing that you would like them to be doing or producing?

Let's go back to the triage nurses in the call-center example a few pages back for an example of how these questions might have ferreted out the actual source of the problem earlier in the process. Note that the example is filled in as if it were from the original conversation about the proposed training. The real issue emerges only gradually as a result of careful questions.

Setting: *Hospital call center requesting customer service training*

How do others view this situation?

Patients are furious when their call is lost and they get kicked out of the system.

Drs are complaining because their patients call our phone nurses incompetent and refuse to talk to anyone but the physician themselves.

Who needs to be involved?

Triage nurses

What will success look like?

Eliminate dropped calls, increase patient satisfaction ratings, minimize complaints to physicians, minimize triage-nurse illnesses.

What has changed in their environment?

Triage nurses call in sick with increasing frequency. When they are out "ill," nurses from family practice or surgery have to pick up the slack, and they don't know the protocols nearly as well.

Added two new obstetricians with huge practices to our clinic.

What other factors might contribute to that result?

Huge increase of calls overall and related to obstetrics specifically.

No modifications to phone system to accommodate the load.

Who else is affected by what participants do?

Physicians and their nurses have to return calls to their angry patients once they get the patient complaints from the switchboard or appointment schedulers. So EVERYONE is affected.

How do you currently measure effectiveness? What analysis have you done so far?

Track number of calls, caller wait times and dropped calls.

Nothing yet on the phone system itself.

What do the triage nurses think might be the issues?

Haven't talked to the triage nurses themselves. They'll probably just complain that they weren't involved in developing the new procedures.

❏ Who is going to be there?

Are you sure you know to whom you are going to present? Even if you know the specific job titles or functions of your intended audience, do you really know what they will expect

For example, the same subject matter might look quite different to customer-facing and internal-facing administrative roles. Will the people working directly with patients have the same concerns about the electronic charting systems as the people in the business office? Will the security or maintenance staffs have the same concerns about customer volume as the sales managers?

It pays to do your prep work before you paint.

Even when you can't access details about your audience before your presentation, you can still adjust when you arrive. Audiences are usually happy to answer questions that help a speaker tailor the message to the people in the room.

Here are a few questions that can help you uncover what your audience is expecting before you step to the podium:

❏ Will management/leadership be included?

❏ How much variation is there within the group?

❏ Will participation be required or optional?

❏ What is the size of the group?

❏ What is their knowledge/experience with the topic?

❏ How formal or informal is the culture? Examples? (e.g. always start on time or wait for latecomers)

Following is an example with what your notes might have looked like if you had been invited to be one of the speakers for those state and county HR directors.

> ### *Social Media Misfire*
>
> The three speakers, including Sheila, had been invited to help Human Resources directors in state and county governments make a belated entry into the world of social media in their work.
>
> The first two speakers were established experts on their topic, and they shared their lessons learned and the hard-won best practices that they had identified. They generously provided examples of sophisticated social-media policies, of staff positions created to use disciplined analytics to "monitor conversations" around their brand, and of tactics for using YouTube videos and Tweets to highlight open positions.
>
> By the time Sheila stepped up to the podium, most of the audience was in a wide-eyed near panic. So a few questions to the group were in order.
>
> It turned out that most of the participants were not entirely sure they had a communications policy of any kind in place, let alone official parameters on the use of social media. At the time of the workshop the vast majority of them were denied access to sites like Facebook, YouTube and even LinkedIn at work, where most of them were one-person departments with no additional staff to assign to social-media strategies. Furthermore, very few in the group had even accessed such sites from home, let alone set up an active account.

So Sheila was able to adjust her presentation accordingly and send participants home with pragmatic, scaled-down action plans they could confidently start the very next day.

Will management/leadership be included?

Audience = leaders from their organizations but not necessarily decision makers.

How much variation is there within the group?

All public HR directors; some from large cities, counties, some from tiny municipal governments and some from State departments.

Will participation be required or optional?

Completely optional, so they are very interested in this hot topic.

What is the size of the group?

Up to 60, including staff from sponsoring organization.

What is the group's knowledge/experience with the topic?

A few individuals use LinkedIn for personal use, but the rest are novices and even in the dark about how to set up profiles, Fan Pages, etc This may be their first exposure.

How formal or informal is the culture? Examples?

Pretty down to earth overall; quite practical and will love any opportunity to talk with peers

❑ What happens afterward?

The challenge before you is to share your expertise in a way that will help bring about a resolution to the problem the sponsor has identified. What else has to be in place back in their environment for your efforts to pay off? Training alone can't change much if nothing else is different when participants return to work.

Even if you were to deliver a powerful session and your participants leave the room eager to try their new skills back on the job, their actual performance will be influenced by dozens of other factors. They are, after all, returning to an environment perfectly suited to getting the result they were getting before attending your session.

Will their colleagues be receptive to the new way you want participants to do things? It's hard to overestimate the impact of an experienced employee saying something like, "Oh, that's what the home office says, but it doesn't work for us. We do it this way instead."

Are supervisors supportive of the new behaviors you are asking of your participants? Will the processes in place expedite or obstruct these behaviors? What if your participants won't be able to apply what you are teaching them for another couple of weeks or a month after your session? What if they might only have a few opportunities to apply it in their whole career?

None of this means you shouldn't provide the workshop. It does, however, affect how you put it together. So your next order of business is to tease out some of the major factors that will affect the ability of your participants to put into practice the things you are teaching them.

Diplomacy with a Sponsor

One of the best phrases we have ever found for suggesting alternatives to a sponsor is, "Have you thought about . . . ?"

Also effective (when the speaker is sincere): "That's interesting. Here's another perspective to consider . . . ."

To be sure of getting attention, show how alternatives could save money: "It might be less expensive and more effective if we . . . ."

Here are some questions to help you do that:

❑ How quickly/How often will participants have an opportunity to use their new behaviors on the job?

❑ How will the new behaviors be reinforced?

❑ What are the consequences to participants if they are successful (or not successful) at implementing the new behaviors?

❑ Who/what are the resources they will be able to access back on the job?

❑ Who else will be affected by what participants will do back on the job? (i.e. systems and processes within the organization; peer support)

❑ What environmental factors might be a barrier to success? What else are they dealing with?

Setting: *New claims system to be used by phone reps*

How quickly/How often will participants have an opportunity to use their new behaviors on the job?

Employees will be required to begin using the new system immediately

How will the new behaviors be reinforced?

Employees will be required to begin using the new system immediately and will be monitored by supervisors listening in on conversations AND verifying appropriate documentation.

What are the consequences to participants if they are successful (or not successful) at implementing the new behaviors?

They are given 30 days to get up to speed or be put on a performance improvement plan. If no changes in the next 10 days, they are subject to discipline and even termination. No particular rewards/incentives are in place for doing well.

Who/what resources will employees be able to access back on the job?

Job aids used in the class would be great. They will have an advisor for the first 30 days. "IT support is great around here."

Who else will be affected by what participants do back on the job?

> *Colleagues have to pick up the slack if they are too slow; time-consuming rework if errors made. Supervisors may have to work 1:1 with them. Ultimately customers will let us know if they aren't satisfied with the responses they receive.*
>
> What environmental factors might be a barrier to success?
>
> *Already short staffed and experiencing a shortage of good applicant candidates for the new-hire training.*
>
> *Existing staffing levels have been fluctuating a lot since the new system was introduced. Many of the older employees have transferred to data entry rather than deal with the complexities of the system. Two supervisors have been promoted to other departments.*

This is a good example of a situation that could be helped a great deal with some well-designed job aids—"cheat sheets" of sorts that users could keep at their workstations. We will cover more about job aids in chapter four.

Formula for Business Results

Training for Impact: How to Link Training to Business Needs and Measure the Results, by Dana Gaines Robinson and James C. Robinson, has a powerful way to illustrate the relative impact of training and the actual work environment.

Learning Experience x Work Environment = Business Results

So if you rate your training like this:		*and the work x environment like this:*		*= you get an impact like this:*
7	x	0	=	0
3	x	2	=	6
2	x	8	=	16

❑ *How will you know if your presentation worked?*

Often "training" sessions conclude with an evaluation form of some kind, sometimes called a "smile sheet," since it tends to capture information like how well participants liked the presenter and the room they were in.

It may also capture a bit about whether participants know things they hadn't before. But even so, this kind of evaluation-form-based measurement rarely correlates very well with the ultimate impact of your presentation on IRACIS, which is (in principle) what you were trying to accomplish in the first place.

Like prepping a room before you paint, figuring out what would constitute evidence that your presentation was effective—well before you even start planning the details—will pay off richly afterward.

For one thing, probing for how the sponsor would be able to measure the impact of your presentation has a way of surfacing really critical potential misunderstandings. Deciding whether to share your expertise to address the issue at hand is as essential as is whether a face to face workshop is the most effective way to deliver it.

Establishing how success will be measured helps get everybody aligned and in agreement about what you are trying to accomplish.

It also goes a long way toward suggesting what types of activities and content belong in your presentation. In essence, it makes designing an effective and relevant "smile sheet" that much easier.

Let's go back to that example of the slowing work efficiency on the fourth floor with the new client records system. You determine that yes, indeed, the issue is a knowledge and skills gap, and you have the expertise they need on fourth floor.

Based on your own experience, you might assume, logically enough, that what the sponsor views as "trouble keeping up" revolves around problem solving with customers. It's tempting to skip validating your assumptions. After all, both you and the sponsor are plenty busy with your "regular" work, and you are both pretty sure you understand each other.

But imagine your surprise if you press to identify what would constitute evidence of a successful presentation, and you discover that the sponsor is really thinking in terms of documentation into a new client-records computer system. What a wildly different kind of workshop that suggests!

Often, if not most of the time, your sponsor will not have given much thought to the business impact of what he or she is asking you to do. The person might even be dismissive or annoyed at the question. Isn't it self evident that there is a knowledge gap and that closing it is a good thing? Does it really have to support IRACIS? It's just a presentation, after all.

Here are some measures that can help your sponsor, skeptical or otherwise, think through the information you need:

❑ What makes this important enough to spend company time and money on training?

❑ How would you describe what this session is intended to achieve to your next-door neighbor?

❑ How will you know the session was successful?

❑ What happens or fails to happen if your session does not achieve its objective? (Bonus: Can you put a dollar value on that?)

❑ If you were a fly on the wall a week after the session, how would you be able to tell the difference between someone who had participated and someone who had not?

❑ What are your people not doing now that you would like them to do?

❑ How would a fly on the wall be able to determine if they started doing this?

❑ What are your people doing now that you would like them to stop doing or do differently?

❑ How would a fly on the wall be able to determine if they had indeed stopped doing this or started doing it differently?

❑ How do you measure this currently?

❑ How else could you measure the impact (on customers, on the business, etc.)?

Setting: *Teaching proper electronic documentation into database.*

What makes this important enough to spend company time and money on training?

Errors end up costing us money and sometimes customers. Takes time for the error to surface, find it, correct it, fill the corrected order, etc. Makes customers upset; they doubt our competence and take their business elsewhere.

How would you describe what this session is intended to achieve to your next-door neighbor?

Decrease errors and omissions in data collection, increase accuracy from 92 percent to 97 percent.

How will you know the session was successful?

Accuracy reports show improvement, fewer correction requests.

If you were a fly on the wall a week after the session, how would you be able to tell the difference between someone who had participated and someone who had not?

What are your people not doing now that you would like them to do?

Not filling in all fields, not double-checking key data, not documenting key elements of interacting with customer still not able to navigate quickly in the system.

How would a fly on the wall be able to determine if they started doing this?

Would see all fields completed; would hear employees confirming key data at end of call while still on the phone with the customer, would hear fewer long silences while employee searches for proper screen.

What are your people doing now that you would like them to stop doing or do differently?

Incurring lengthy phone conversations with a great deal of silence while they search out information for customers. Also, many calls remain undocumented based on the call queue, so there is no follow up when clients call back based on insufficient or even; inaccurate information given the first time.

How would a fly on the wall be able to determine if they had indeed stopped doing this or started doing it differently?

Would hear fewer long silences; would see fewer calls related to inaccurate/insufficient data; would see more thorough documentation of initial calls, which makes subsequent calls more efficient/effective.

How do you measure this currently?

Automatic reports on categories of calls, lengths of calls.

How else could you measure the impact (on customers, on the business, etc.)?

Customer-service surveys do not include complaints related to data-entry errors & omissions.

Chapter 1

How Might Your Presentation Impact the Following?

Increase Revenue   IRACIS

- Average product or service sale
- Billable hours
- Cross or upsell volume
- Customer or employee referrals
- Increased productivity
- New product/service launches
- New clients
- Orders placed or claims processed
- Time to market
- Total Sales Volume
- Volume of new accounts
- Down time reduction
- Projects completed on time and under budget
- Improve equipment efficiencies
- Improve availability/reliability

Avoid Costs   IRACIS

- Absenteeism rate
- Average product defects
- Capital expenses
- Commuting time
- Compensation for comp, harassment, grievances
- Cost of Claims
- Cost of disability accommodations
- Employee retention rate
- Error rates
- Expenses
- Administrative
- Healthcare/Medical
- Legal
- Office/Supplies
- Payroll
- Product Development
- Sales/Marketing
- Technology
- Avoid fines (regulatory compliance)
- Training
- Workers' Compensation
- Injuries or safety violations
- Project completion on time

Improve Service   IRACIS

- Repeat business from existing clients
- Referrals to others from existing clients
- Customer Satisfaction Surveys
- POS SurveyData
- Customer loyalty
- Customer complaints
- Increase usage-service department
- Customer returns
- Inventory adjustments
- Repair time
- Employee loyalty
- Increased use of service online
- FAQ page hits
- Online problem resolution hits

Critical (Though Not-So-Typical) Metrics

- Brand recognition or awareness
- Caliber of job candidates
- Community Image or Relations
- Commitment to action
- Complete documentation
- Customer engagement or satisfaction
- Diversity of applicants
- Improved ataff Morale
- Employee effectiveness
- Employee engagement or satisfaction
- Enhanced teamwork
- Participant confidence

the *Engaging* **Expert**   Begin with the End in Mind   **21**

Consulting Questions

Prep work

- Why is this presentation (or workshop/training/etc.) really necessary in the first place?
- How does it support IRACIS, goddess of business objectives?
- Is it really a transfer-of-knowledge issue?
- Who is going to be there?
- What happens afterward?
- How will you know it worked?

The Busines Case for training

- Why does management care about this?
- How much is this problem really costing, directly and indirectly?
- What are your customers concerned about?
- What makes this urgent enough to spend company time, money and other resources on it?

Will training will really address the problem at hand:?

- What are you hoping to achieve? How can that be measured?
- Have participants done this successfully in the past? If yes, what has changed? (e.g. new equipment, new processes, new state mandates, etc.)
- What specifically are participants doing now?
- What happens if we do nothing?
- What are the Real World consequences to individuals if they are not successful? What are the rewards to the individual for outstanding performance? (How do you know people know these?)
- Who else is affected by what participants do as a result of this session? Would they be able to tell the difference if someone had or had not participated? How?

Suggesting Alternatives

- How do others view this situation?
- What has changed in their environment?
- What have you tried in the past?
- Who needs to be involved?
- Who else is affected by what participants do?
- What other factors might contribute to that result?
- How do you currently measure effectiveness? What analysis have you done so far?
- What will success look like?

What your audience is expecting

- ❑ Will management/leadership be included?
- ❑ How much variation is there within the group?
- ❑ Will participation be required or optional?
- ❑ What is the size of the group?
- ❑ What is their knowledge/experience with the topic?
- ❑ How formal or informal is the culture? Examples?

Factors that will affect putting into practice the things you are teaching them.

- ❑ How quickly/How often will participants have an opportunity to use their new behaviors on the job?
- ❑ How will the new behaviors be reinforced?
- ❑ What are the consequences to participants if they are successful (or not successful) at implementing the new behaviors?
- ❑ Who/what are the resources they will be able to access back on the job?
- ❑ Who else will be affected by what participants will do back on the job? (i.e. systems and processes within the organization; peer support)
- ❑ What environmental factors might be a barrier to success? What else are they dealing with?

Measures to help your sponsor think through the information you need.

- ❑ What makes this important enough to spend time and money on training?
- ❑ How would you describe what this session is intended to achieve to your next-door neighbor?
- ❑ How will you know the session was successful?
- ❑ What happens or fails to happen if your session does not achieve its objective? (Bonus: Can you put a dollar value on that?)
- ❑ If you were a fly on the wall a week after the session, how would you be able to tell the difference between someone who had participated and someone who had not?
    - ❖ What are your people not doing now that you would like them to do?
    - ❖ How to determine if they started doing this?
    - ❖ What are your people doing now that you would like them to stop doing or do differently?
    - ❖ How would a fly on the wall be able to determine if they had indeed stopped doing this or started doing it differently?
- ❑ How do you measure this currently?
- ❑ How else could you measure the impact?

Congratulations! If you collect answers to even a fraction of the preceding questions, you are waaaaaay ahead of most experts in your position. With a clear picture of the end you have in mind, you are now ready to put together some rehearsal opportunities that will help your message affect real change.

Rehearsals – opportunities to practice the way you want participants to perform back in their work environment – are critical if you are serious about helping your participants absorb what you are teaching them.

Doing new things, or even doing old things a new way, takes practice. Your participants will practice with you in your session or without you back on the job.

CREATE REHEARSAL OPPORTUNITIES

"Learning is an active process. We learn by doing. Only knowledge that is used sticks in your mind."

– Dale Carnegie,

"It is my experience over the last 30 years that if people do not practice what they learned in the classroom, they will not use it when they leave."

– Deb Laurel

Words Are Not Enough

They say the most seductive words in the English language are, "I'd like your opinion about ...." And when you are an expert or a specialist tasked with teaching other people about what you know, the siren song of your own voice can be astonishingly seductive.

It's nothing you intend, of course. You're passionate about your topic. After all, you invested quite a bit of time and energy to learn what you know. And naturally you want to help people avoid many of the mistakes you made along the way.

So you explain as much as you can in the time you have, trying to squeeze as much helpful information into the session as the clock allows. But the more you try to help, the less they seem to learn. How maddening!

It turns out that when you are trying to teach others, the most effective way to get your expertise out of your head is not via your mouth, or even via your written words.

The most effective way to get your expertise out of your head is to create experiences for the people you are teaching.

For one thing, you probably don't even recognize all the stuff you know. Many of the nuances have long since become so automatic that you're no longer aware of them; you take them for granted as an obvious given.

Skeptical? Imagine yourself in the passenger seat trying to teach a complete novice how to drive. Could you really describe all the subtle things you do as a matter of course when you drive? When you press on the accelerator or the brake, how much pressure is too much or too little? How do you convey the "feel" of the best moment to hit the clutch and change gears?

That gap between what you know how to do and what you can actually explain is the difference between *procedural* knowledge and *declarative* knowledge. Most presentations and training sessions address only declarative knowledge, which is generally insufficient to induce lasting changes in performance.

So what is an expert or specialist to do? You can't dump your procedural knowledge into someone else's head.

But you *can* create targeted experiences – rehearsal opportunities – for your learners. Isolate a key concept to convey, then pour the richness of your procedural knowledge into creating ways for your learners to practice it – preferably ways that mimic the Real World where they will be applying what you teach them.

In the case of your novice driver, you might find an empty parking lot or little-used country road where he or she can safely practice accelerating and braking without simultaneously worrying about turn signals and cross traffic and the hundreds of other details demanding a driver's attention.

In a case of, say, training new convenience-store managers, you can provide simplified scenarios that help them practice making key choices. Then gradually add more and more of the variables at play in the Real World. As an experienced convenience-store manager, you know these variables and their significance better than anyone. You know which details will create that certain "feel" you get when you need to take action.

It's not easy, of course, to stand back and let people practice – making mistakes and figuring out how to correct them with only minimal intervention from you. You want to help! And they want you to help them. "I'd like your opinion about …."

But in sharing your expertise, only a portion of what you know can get out of your head with words. Let your expertise out by creating targeted experiences, where much more of the richness of what you don't realize you know can be absorbed by the people you teach.

It's Not About You

You may be a brilliant orator. Your product might have the capacity to bring about world peace. You probably have terrific insights to share.

But that's not what matters to your audience.

Possibly the single most impactful concept to remember when you are sharing your expertise with others is the ol' WIIFM: "What's In It For Me?" That's the filter your learners automatically apply to every word you speak, every slide you show, every aspect of your session.

When your objective is to affect how your participants perform back in the Real World, you place a high priority on framing your content in the way it will have the most impact rather than what is most comfortable for you.

As the saying goes, "I like ice cream. But when I go fishing I use worms, 'cause fish like worms."

Pop Quiz!

If your house is burning down, what do you want the firefighters to do?

a) Describe the principal methods for dousing house fires.

b) Put out the fire.

Focus on the Action

In the Real World, how can you tell if someone really "knows" or "understands" something?

Unless you have psychic abilities you aren't telling anyone about, all you can do is observe their actions—their performance.

You can *hear* someone interacting with a customer in a way that reflects understanding of your content. You can *see* people doing a procedure in the correct sequence.

When you are trying to create targeted experiences for your learners, it's tricky to stay focused on specific, observable behaviors, and remarkably easy to slip back into the comfortable ambiguity of "become aware of" and similarly vague language. One way to stay on target is figure out how you would prove that your objective was met.

Imagine you are before a judge and jury providing evidence that your participants do indeed "know" or "understand" what you taught them.

What would you invoke as your proof?

Those are the behaviors you want people to practice in your session. Those become the starting point for creating targeted experiences that mimic the Real World of your learners.

Perspective of a Fly on the Wall

Imagine you are a fly on the wall watching two people go about their work. One of them attended a workshop you led; the other did not.

How do you determine which is which?

As a fly you cannot read minds. You can only observe behavior. The only way to tell if a person *knows* the procedures you taught is to see him following the procedures. The only way to determine whether a person *understands* how to establish empathy with a customer is to observe her interacting with the customer.

It's tempting to settle for abstractions like "they will know…" or "they will understand…" when you are figuring out how your participants will use what you teach them.

Don't.

Pretend you are that skeptical fly on the wall, looking for proof of what your participants can actually *DO* before and after you share your expertise.

Let's see how this looks in a few examples. What would an outside observer see that would make clear someone had absorbed what you shared?

What you are teaching	Someone who learned it	Someone who hasn't
Customer service in a retail setting	Greeted each customer with immediate eye contact, a smile and a question like, "How can I help you?" Recognized each customer who used the store's credit card at the register by saying enthusiastically, "Thank you for being one of our valued customers!" Asked, "Were you able to find everything you needed?" at the beginning of each interaction at the Point Of Sale (POS).	Avoided eye contact and responded only when customers asked for help. Ignored the method of payment when checked each customer out. Did not initiate conversation with any customer at the POS.
Product training for sales representatives	With each customer interaction, outlined the two most important benefits of the new, improved version following the succinct descriptions on the job aid. Completed all but the "authorized initials" box on each new account in the system and sent a duplicate to the team lead by 5pm. each day. Increased daily new-account calls by 50% in the first week following new product training.	Stated the standard features of the old product when explaining the new version in all customer conversations. Completed a written file for each new account added with an email summary to the team lead at the end of the third day. Maintained daily new-account call volume from previous month.
Orientation in a manufacturing environment	Located the appropriate safety equipment when confronted with a potentially hazardous chemical on the floor. Looked confused upon opening a parts' carton. Checked the XYZ process flow on the job aid posted at the lead's desk, then unpacked the carton, placing the materials in the appropriate bin. Completed a timecard at the end of the shift and signed the back before replacing in the rack of staff cards.	Asked a co worker what to do when confronted with a potentially hazardous chemical on the floor. Asked several others what to do with cartons of materials delivered to the site. Exited the shop floor at the end of the shift neglecting to stop at the timecard rack.

Identify the DO

Given your own long experience with your topic, it's probably not as difficult as you might expect to come up with a list of specific, observable behaviors that could be practiced in rehearsal activities.

Identify the Most Impactful

When you identify the behaviors you want your learners to practice, you could end up with a really long list. When that happens, prioritize the one or two behaviors that will have the greatest impact on performance.

You will find a treasure trove of raw materials for rehearsal opportunities by simply scanning your own memory (and perhaps that of other experts) for common errors and horror stories, for what went right in success stories and what went entirely wrong in disasters.

Here are a few additional questions that can help you dig down to the specific behaviors you want from your participants after they learn from you.

- ❑ What event triggered the request for a presentation or training?
- ❑ What does proficiency look like? What do you see when you watch a proficient employee? (How much? How fast? How good?)
- ❑ What are the typical issues people are faced with? Where do they come up?
- ❑ What are some of the common mistakes people are making now?
- ❑ What are customers complaining about?
- ❑ What are the variations that arise? Distractions? Extenuating circumstances?
- ❑ What resources or job aids do they already have? Which ones do they really use?

The answers you get will point you to which Real-World experiences you want to recreate in your session.

The trickier part is figuring out *how* to bring that Real World vividly to life within the confines of a classroom, lecture hall or conference room.

The following example is part of the discussion leading up to the training example described on page 104, "Managing Money Not Their Own."

> Setting: A *non-profit organization wants training for its volunteers who handle money*
>
> What event triggered the request for a presentation?
>
> *An accusation of theft triggered a long, expensive investigation that ultimately found not theft but very sloppy record keeping.*
>
> What does proficiency look like? What do you see when you watch a proficient employee? (How much? How fast? How good?)
>
> *Volunteers always collect receipts and make quick, adequate notes on them to make it easy to code them for their year-end report. They use multiple lines in their checkbook from the organization to record critical details about expenditures. They can produce complete, accurate records of the money entrusted to them at any time, and they submit a complete, accurate financial summary at the end of the year.*

What are the typical issues people are faced with? Where do they come up?

Volunteers are not sure how to document how money moves through the accounts they are responsible for. They volunteer because they want to work with people, not because they like record keeping. They are also busy with other things like full-time jobs and family life. Taking the time to document things as they come up seems burdensome to them.

What are some of the common mistakes people are making now?

They forget to collect receipts and to make adequately detailed notes of deposits and expenditures as they come up; then they try to reconstruct everything at the end of the year.

What are customers complaining about?

Volunteers don't know what the guidelines are for handling money on behalf of the organization. No single resource exists where they can easily find all the information they need in one place.

What are the variations that arise? Distractions? Extenuating circumstances?

Volunteers often code receipts and expenditures inaccurately. Often volunteers are managing groups of people at the times they are spending or receiving money for the organization. When a volunteer has to leave partway through the year, accurate records are often not available to a successor volunteer.

What resources or job aids do they already have? Which ones do they really use?

They have the manual on policies and procedures for the organization, but it was not updated to reflect the changes in banking brought about by the Patriot Act. Separate, piecemeal memos went out to volunteers about various changes caused by the new law. Some volunteers have made and shared their own "quick reference" sheets to code receipts; they keep these in the checkbook they have for the organization.

What About Abstract Qualities?

What if you are asked to deliver a session on something like "leadership" or "organization"? How do you dig down to specific, observable behaviors associated with such broad concepts?

Try framing your question in terms of results. "What is the result of being a good leader?" "What is the result of good organization skills?"

Mimic the Real World

Let's go back to our driving example. Think about how *you* learned to drive. You were taught about the rules of the road and some general principles about driving, and you even passed a written test about driving. But could you have taken a car across town by yourself at that point?

You didn't *really* learn how to drive until you got behind the wheel. You experimented with how much force you should use to hit the brakes and how quickly to turn the steering wheel. You made mistakes and got useful feedback — both from whoever was in the passenger seat and from simply experiencing the consequences of your actions.

Of course, you would not have wanted to learn those things in rush-hour traffic.

You needed a simplified version of reality behind the wheel, a place where there were fewer variables to keep track of, where it was safe to experiment and make mistakes, and where you could practice in a structured way. This is exactly what your learners need from you.

Notice all the action verbs in that last paragraph: *practice, make mistakes, experiment, keep track.*

The key is to base your activities on the same types of decisions, choices and actions that will be asked of your learners back in the environment in which they will apply what you share.

That's worth repeating, because it's really, really important.

The key is to base your activities on the same types of decisions, choices and actions that will be asked of your learners back in the environment in which they will apply what you share.

If the use of the word "activities" makes you nervous, here's some good news: Rehearsals can happen in the mind as well as in physical actions. Story telling, discussing scenarios and even playing appropriate games can all be forms of practice.

How Many "Chunks" of Information Can You Hold in Working Memory?

Based on George Miller's classic 1956 study, it was believed we can hold 7 -/+ 2 items in our head. The new research suggests 2-4 (at the most) for chunks in our working memory.

> ### Abstraction Is the Luxury of the Expert
>
> "Novices perceive concrete details as concrete details. Experts perceive concrete details as symbols of patterns and insights that they have learned through years of experience. And, because they are capable of seeing a higher level of insight, they naturally want to talk on a higher level. They want to talk about chess strategies, not about bishops moving diagonally. [...] Abstraction demands some concrete foundation. Trying to teach an abstract principle without concrete foundations is like trying to start a house by building the roof in the air."
>
> Chip Heath and Dan Heath
>
> *Make It Stick*

Scenarios Big and Small

The most straightforward way to mimic the Real World is to use scenarios. You can make them as complex as a large case study or as simple as a carefully framed multiple-choice question.

Multiple Choice

If you make the choices reflect the real judgment calls or decisions your learners will have to make on the job, a multiple-choice question really can vividly evoke the dilemmas of the Real World.

> **Slow Start for a New Employee**
>
> Your new direct report, Tom, is not hitting his targets. Both you and he are frustrated, and you seem to be seeing less and less of him. Which of the following best matches what you would do?
>
> a) Accurately document his performance issues.
> b) Assign Tom a "mentor" to help get him up to speed.
> c) Ask your own supervisor for advice.
> d) Apologize to Tom for not providing adequate initial support.

> ### *Handling Pushback*
>
> Your boss wants you to do a training session on some new compliance rules, and she is pushing back when you press for details on the "DO" she hopes to see back in the Real World. Which question is most likely to give you the information you need for creating rehearsal opportunities?
>
> a) What are the likely consequences to individuals and to the company if we fail to comply with the new rules?
>
> b) So you just want me to do an information dump on the new regulations?
>
> c) Would it be more cost effective in the long run if we put a summary on the company intranet rather than taking so many people off the line for an hour?

Branching Scenario

If you string a series of multiple-choice options together, you can create a branching scenario.

Insubordination

A respectful workplace session for municipal employees starts off a branching scenario with a brief description:

"Carla and Jerome have both applied for a promotion to police sergeant. After the recruitment process is complete, Carla is awarded the job. Jerome feels that he was more qualified, and that Carla only received the promotion because she is female. Consequently he lets everyone know he thinks it's unfair, and he files a formal complaint. Jerome also refuses to follow Carla's instructions and is disciplined for it. As a fellow police officer, what would you do?"

The group chooses among three possible actions on a PowerPoint slide:

a. Ignore it. Jerome is probably right.

b. Take Jerome aside and say, "Whether she got it fairly or not, she is still your sergeant. If you don't knock it off, you'll end up getting in trouble."

c. Comment to a group of friends at work on what an idiot Jerome is being. "Doesn't he know he could get nailed for retaliation??"

Let's say the group chooses the first option, ignoring it. When the participant clicks on the option, the slide jumps to a new situation that results from that choice, and three more options appear for how to act in the new circumstances: "A call comes in from dispatch about an accident, and because Jerome didn't follow orders, he did not come in as scheduled. The dispatcher frantically calls you to cover for him."

a. Don't say anything to Jerome. These things happen, and it's not your problem.

b. Request reassignment so you don't have this situation again.

c. Approach Jerome privately and point out, "Your behavior is making things hard for the rest of us."

The group selects from among the new options, and clicking on it jumps the slide to an updated situation based on the choice; and once more there are three options that reflect the possibilities in the new circumstances.

Case Study

As the example above shows, a snippet as short as a few sentences can provide the raw material for a rich discussion of appropriate actions in the Real World of your participants.

Of course, your participants probably have a rich store of experiences of their own that you could draw on. Why not have them describe to a partner or small group some specific incidents they have observed or experienced, and have the group come up with alternative ways of dealing with the problem?

Uncovering Nuances Learned from Experience

As a table group, create a list of the many ways you've learned the complexities of this company's markets, its services and reputation *while on the job*.

Pooling Lessons Learned

Choose someone you've just met at this session, and then explain how *you* have launched an installation project similar to the one before us.

> ### *Learning Coaching Skills*
>
> Turn to a partner and share a time that you received less than positive feedback in a performance evaluation. Without a lot of detail, describe about how you felt on the receiving end and how you might have done it differently.

What sort of scenario might you use in your next presentation that helps your learners think through the consequences of their choices in the Real World?

Simulations

Simulations can take many forms, from reacting verbally to a scenario to elaborate machinery like a flight simulator. The first-aid-training mentioned a few pages ago makes extensive use of mini-simulations, with mannequins that mimic real human bodies and with verbal descriptions of specific conditions and what is happening as a result of a given choice.

> ### *City-Wide Disaster Drills*
>
> Gathered in the room were fire fighters, police officers, street-maintenance staff and communications staff. Their purpose was to practice how they would respond to special events, such as a dignitary visiting the city. With paper documents and maps they worked through issues like crowd control, public notification to avoid a specific area, medical issues that could arise, and harnessing potential panic.

Break Down the Component Parts

What is the smallest task that is part of a key concept you want to teach? Can you identify one or a few irreducible elements that are essential to a particular practice? Allow your learners to practice those things in isolation, then gradually add more variables that get closer and closer to the Real World in which they will be using the skill.

> ### Bank Teller Training
>
> One of the key responsibilities of bank tellers is to verify whether a check is negotiable or not. If it is missing a date or an endorsement, for example, it cannot be cashed. In their training for new tellers a major bank demonstrates a methodical technique to verify that all six of the critical elements are present on a check. Participants get to practice several times determining whether sample checks are negotiable.
>
> Then in snapshots more variables are added. Here is a picture of a customer and a speech balloon of their request. Now not only does the learner have to verify that the check is negotiable, but also determine, say, whether to request ID, whether to use a UV scanner or check scanner, and whether there is anything about the customer that prompts them to ask additional questions.

Learning First Aid and CPR

To earn certification in basic first aid and CPR (Cardio-Pulmonary Resuscitation), participants need to be able to determine whether and how to provide life-saving interventions in a variety of circumstances. Possibly the most critical is the assessment phase, in which the first aider checks for consciousness, breathing and circulation. So they practice just that part several times until they are comfortable with it.

Then they learn and practice the technique for dealing with a particular condition that they might find, like rescue breathing for example. They practice it as part of a guided scenario – starting with the assessment, just as they would in real life. As learners check the mannequin in the (imaginary) context, the instructor describes at each step what they find so they can react to it appropriately.

Each new intervention technique they learn is added to the mix of possible outcomes in the practice scenarios. By the end of the course the range of conditions they might have to respond to in these guided scenarios is quite substantial.

Other Ways to Rehearse

Role Play

The words can strike terror into the hearts of some participants – largely because the first thing that comes to mind is two or more hapless "volunteers" acting out a situation in front of the whole group.

In fact, you can get a lot more mileage out of "role play" activities in much less demanding ways.

For one thing, instead of singling out a couple of individuals to suffer while the rest of the group remains passive, try grouping people in pairs or triads and have everyone working at once.

Triads, by the way, are typically used when one of the three is assigned the role of listening to the interaction between the other two and providing feedback in some form.

You can provide very little or a lot of structure to role-play activities. Below are two highly scripted examples.

> ### *Perspectives on a Merger*
>
> At a large meeting to explain the details of a pending merger, participants were asked to open a sealed envelope that had been inserted randomly in their handouts. Inside was simply the name of one of a half-dozen types of positions in the company. Participants were asked to think from the perspective of someone in that role and identify at least three likely concerns and three potential positives about the merger. Then they shared their lists in small groups.
>
> Since the audience included people from a variety of positions throughout the company, this exercise helped surface perspectives that people had not previously considered.

For the following example each person in a pair got a different part of the scenario. They then practiced applying some of the project-management skills they were learning in the class.

Project: Paint interior on the main floor of a house about to go on the market

Project Sponsor: Homeowner

Project Manager: Good friend who offered to help by handling some of the painting

You are the: Homeowner/Project Sponsor

Your overall goal ("corporate goal"):

Have the house ready to list for sale within two months

Factors that could affect QUALITY/SCOPE:

You need to paint the living room and the dining room, totaling just shy of 400 square feet.

- You would also like to paint the entry foyer and kitchen bringing the total to right around 600 square feet.
- You do not plan to paint the back hall or half bathroom on the main floor.

Factors that could affect TIME/SCHEDULE:

- New carpet will be laid in the living room in just over two weeks.
- Your neighbor's two teenagers are willing to help for $8 hour.

Factors that could affect BUDGET/COST:

- You think you should be able to handle all of the main floor painting for $300, so that is how much you have budgeted for it. You don't remember how you came up with that figure, but altering it substantially would disrupt other plans for getting the house ready to sell.

Other factors:

- The living room is currently painted in vivid, saturated jewel tones. Your realtor insists it needs to be a much more subdued, neutral color to sell the house.

- You just discovered last week that an extremely clever squirrel has been trying to build a nest in the fireplace, and he has been dragging off paintbrushes and other small objects, apparently for that purpose.

Project: Paint interior on the main floor of a house about to go on the market

Project Sponsor: Homeowner

Project Manager: Good friend who offered to help by handling some of the painting

You are the: Good friend/Project Manager

Factors that could affect QUALITY/SCOPE:

- You have very high standards, since you worked summers as a painter in college.

Factors that could affect TIME/SCHEDULE:

- You are potentially available to help during evenings and weekends.
- You have an all-day family commitment next Saturday.
- You are leaving in three weeks for a 10-day business trip in France.

Factors that could affect BUDGET/COST:

- You happen to know that a gallon of paint costs roughly $30 and covers approximately 300 square feet, depending on the color it is covering.

- You believe that the paint the homeowner plans to purchase is advertised as one-coat paint.

- Your brother is available to help out for a couple of days as a favor.

- Last time you had to purchase all the supplies – brushes, rollers, edge tape, drop cloths, etc. – it came to about $300.

- You prefer to use some of your own equipment, such as the swell, brand-new professional paintbrush set you just got as a gift.

Other factors:

- You have a passionate aversion to the color beige; just looking at it makes you feel queasy.

> ### What Constitutes "Active"?
>
> "Response can take the form of answering a question, filling in a blank, labeling something, solving a problem, making a decision, or even discussing and arguing. It can take any form that elicits an active response to the learning content."
>
> So which of these is most accurate?
>
> a) Learners learn better if the response they emit is out loud or written down – an overt response.
>
> b) Learners learn better if the response they emit is in their heads – a silent or covert response.
>
> c) Learners learn better if they respond. There is no significant difference between overt or covert responding.
>
> Correct answer: c "… what the research shows is that active responding is the critical ingredient. What is also important is that the response be a meaningful one."
>
> Harold Stolovitch & Erica Keeps
Telling Ain't Training

Storytelling

Stories can be a form of rehearsal when they help learners imagine *applying* new concepts *in context*.

Highly technical or dry content can become more meaningful by orders of magnitude when embedded in a story.

Stories anchor learning. Our brains are wired for stories, so they are particularly powerful tools for helping people learn.

> *Jane Bozarth, author of several books on learning, gives several examples of transforming dry data into stories with sticking power in her regular column, Nuts and Bolts, in Learning Solutions Magazine. The following excerpt from an eLearning course is reprinted with permission.*
>
> The trick is to get away FROM just delivering data and to get TO developing an interesting treatment for the content instead. For instance:
>
>> *From this*: "Facts about the Cascade" – For UK-based veterinarians, circumstances under which they may use drugs not formally approved. Screens [in an eLearning course] provide details about the policy and a printable "do/do not" job aid.
>>
>> *To this*: "The Gamekeeper's Conundrum" – Provide an overview of the Cascade prior to accessing the eLearning course. Challenge: Faced with an angry farmer whose partridges are dying, the new field veterinarian must correctly decide whether conditions warrant administering a non-approved drug.
>
> Another example:
>
>> *From this*: "Reporting Harassment: The Supervisor's Role" – Screens outline circumstances, rules for, and

processes required in reporting unlawful workplace harassment. Program includes multiple-choice and true/false assessments.

To this: "It's About Richard" – Using still images and audio voiceover, a stressed employee comes to her supervisor (the learner) to report harassment by a co-worker. The learner must choose appropriate supervisory responses as the situation escalates.

And yet a final example:

From this: "World Hunger" – Slides of facts and data about world hunger, including some interactive maps.

To this: "Hunger Banquet: A Seat at the Table" – User is offered a choice of cases to review. Each case focuses on one person dealing with hunger in his/her own environment and culture. Cases include the person's full name, a brief biography, and the reality of life for the person, often struggling against impossible obstacles. Facts and data are built in alongside the main portion of content. (See http://www.oxfamamerica.org/multimedia/flash/a-seat-at-the-table)

What do the "*To this*" examples have in common? In every instance, a designer took dry, static content and found an engaging storyline, a meaningful context in which to situate the content. In two of the three instances here, the story asks learners to make decisions and experience the consequences; in the third, there are dire consequences for the case subjects.

> It's frustrating that some people view the word "story" as "soft and squishy." So let's try some other words: Narrative. Detailed case. Contextual example. Scenario. Diegesis. There are no cutesy fairy tales in the examples here. "A Seat at the Table," for instance, offers vivid realistic details about humans who are struggling to live.
>
> excerpted from "Nuts and Bolts: What's Your Story?"
> Learning Solutions Magazine, Aug. 2, 2011

Action Planning

Be sure your message includes a specific call to action, and give participants an opportunity to make a detailed plan for carrying it out. This provides another opportunity to rehearse new behavior before implementing it in the Real World.

Your action planning can be as simple as asking partners to share their responses to a question along the lines of, "List three specific things you will do differently as a result of what you learned today." Or you could add that question to your evaluation form if you use one.

In general, the more substantial or complex the behavior change you are asking for, the more detailed you should make your action-planning activities.

Divide and Conquer

Ask half of the table groups in your session to identify potential barriers to integrating your process or procedure into their Real World. Ask the other half of the table groups to identify ways to immediately integrate the new process or procedure into their Real World.

You could ask volunteers to share one or more items on their lists with the whole group, and then give everyone an opportunity to react to them. Or have the two halves of the room trade lists, so the barriers groups could identify potential stumbling blocks to integration and the integration groups could identify solutions to the potential barriers.

Give Every Presentation a Clear Call to Action

"But I'm just giving a little speech," you might say. "Why would I need a call to action?"

On the other hand, why are you taking the time to share your expertise if you don't expect it to impact your audience in some way? (They are, after all, listening for the WIIFM – "what's in it for me?")

> Don't leave this to chance. Don't assume your audience will be able to deduce what probably seems obvious to you. Their brains are already busy just digesting what you have shared. So make it easier for them to act on their newfound knowledge by spelling out specifically what you want them to do.
>
> That specificity is important. An experiment on encouraging university students to take part in a food drive for charity showed that giving explicit instructions can give a tremendous boost to the response rate. One group of students received a letter asking them to give a can of food to a booth on Tresidder Plaza (a well-known spot on the campus). A second group of students received a more detailed letter including a map and a specific request for a can of beans. The general letter got a response rate of four percent; just over 33 percent gave food after receiving the detailed letter.
>
> So as professional speaker and speaking coach Olivia Mitchell advises, "In your presentations, take people through the detailed steps they'll need to take, and give them all the information they need to carry through in a handout."

Use the Real "Real World"

Which tools from the actual Real World of your learners could be brought into the room where you are teaching? Using existing documents and resources not only saves you time and effort, but they are generally more impactful for participants. And you can't mimic the Real World any better than having your learners use the very resources they would turn to anyway back in their usual environment.

Do your participants have smart phones or laptops? Put people to work digging for relevant information they can apply in your session.

BYOT (Bring Your Own Technology)

At a conference break-out session on social media in the workplace, the facilitator observed the number of laptops in the room. So he started one of his activities by saying, "Since you already have laptops, get into small groups with at least one laptop per group. Now find some of the resources you will need in order to establish a social-media policy at your own workplace, like samples of policies other companies are using."

Using Company Intranet for Company Training

A major accounting firm offered training to experienced practitioners who were asked to serve as coaches for more junior employees. The company intranet had extensive resources for the role, but few coaches had ever explored it. So many of the activities Terri and Sheila designed for the session required that participants find and apply those resources to practice specific skills.

For example, participants got to prepare for specific aspects of upcoming annual reviews with their actual individual protégés, identifying possible promotion

> tracks and choices of assignments for each. They used checklists on the company intranet to help them plan for and schedule regular communication with their protégés, and to script real feedback conversations for those who were underperforming.

You don't need to go high-tech to bring Real-World resources into your session. There are plenty of books and printed articles (professional and otherwise) out there that participants could turn to in their particular circumstances.

> ### Instant Leadership Training
>
> Internationally recognized training guru and author, Sivasailam "Thiagi" Thiagarajan, describes a highly successful leadership workshop that relied on leadership books from best-seller lists, hardly any of which he had read.
>
> Participants each selected a book of their choice and took 20 minutes to glean six key ideas from it that they could apply the very next day if necessary. Then they took 20 minutes to explain the six principles they had identified to a partner. Then the pairs took 20 minutes to explain their combined 12 principles to another pair, bringing their total to 24 key ideas.

In the next 20 minutes foursomes identified the single best idea out of their 24 and presented it to the whole group. And in the final 20 minutes each participant chose one of the principles that had been described and explained to a partner specifically how they planned to use it to address a real issue they were currently facing.

Thiagi's Observations About the Instant Leadership Training Session

- It was no accident that this methodology he chose relies on using leadership skills during the session.

- When groups found that some of the key concepts they had identified showed up in multiple books, that's good! It must be a valid principle. When groups found ideas that conflicted, that's good! Let's discuss under what circumstances each of them would be appropriate.

- While he is sought after by major corporations around the world, Thiagi notes that even more important than his own expertise is the fact that "learners believe their own data."

The ultimate example of bringing the Real World into the classroom is to have participants do real work – the kind that generates revenue for the business or in some other way satisfies IRACIS.

Generate Real Orders

A large retail store was teaching new marketing staff to generate copy for direct-mail advertising. For the final exercise participants created an actual direct-mail piece that was sent to 1,000 actual potential customers. If the mailing resulted in six or more orders, the creator passed the course.

Helping the Sales Force

A technology company got extra mileage out of its product training for its sales representatives. For their final project, participants drafted a real proposal for a real client of the company. The proposals were reviewed not just by the person leading the session but also by an actual sales manager, who would add feedback to make the proposal ready to send to the client.

Developing Company Service Standards

A newly formed service department team was brought together as a result of merger between two companies. As part of the customer-service training for the new business, participants drafted the service standards to be used enterprise wide.

Performance Impact Model

The lynchpin of the whole idea of creating rehearsal opportunities is the direct, unambiguous connection to IRACIS in the Real World.

Since you spent the time and great effort to confirm the business value for your presentation (and you reached agreement with your sponsor on the realistic impact it should have), the most relevant behaviors should start to become clear when you link your presentation to IRACIS.

Notice some of the key details of this model:

- ***Every element*** *of the model is connected to and supports IRACIS. Anything that does not clearly connect to the larger structure is not necessary.*

- *The most distinctive element of the model is the rehearsal opportunities, shown here as an actor rehearsing. These are chances for participants to practice the specific, observable behaviors that produce the business results you are after.*

- *Detailed information to include is the last element to consider. Any information that is not absolutely necessary for successful rehearsal is left out.*

The nice thing about making sure your presentation supports IRACIS is that she provides a beautifully clear lens to focus your content.

Let's use a call center as a quick example of how to apply the Performance Impact Model.

Call-center training		
	Step 1: Identify specifically how your presentation will support IRACIS. What resulting improvements in performance will provide more value for the organization than it costs to provide the session? How will that be measured?	• Improve customer satisfaction scores (Improve Service) by reducing call wait time average to under two minutes
	Step 2: Identify the specific, observable behaviors that will produce that result.	• Use the system efficiently and accurately • Discern customer needs quickly • Escalate to next level appropriately
	Step 3: Create rehearsal opportunities that use those behaviors.	• Use the system to address specific sample scenarios that require a variety of different screens • Generate open-ended questions that help surface customer needs • Create a flow chart of situations requiring referral to the next level
	Step 4: Identify what participants really, *really* need to know to rehearse successfully.	• Customer Contact items required and what screens to document these in the system • Standards and procedure to escalate calls • Best Practices on navigating multiple screens during calls?

If you still have a lot of content you are tempted to include, you may want to go on to identify which bits are *not* strictly necessary for successful practice of target behaviors. In this case that might include things like procedures that are needed only a few times a year, or trying to address every conceivable variation learners could face, or how to generate and analyze management reports on the system.

Pick a few of the things with the greatest potential to have noticeable consequences, and put them in an appendix or job aid.

This model probably turns your usual sequence of developing content on its head. You start with the end result and work backwards to the content. Everything turns on figuring out the specific actions you want to see from your learners back in their natural habitat.

Here's another example of how to use the Performance Impact Model. A national company asked Sheila to speak to a large group on the topic of stress management at work as part of a wellness initiative. The initiative was precipitated by not one but two recent (and painful) rounds of layoffs.

Stress-Management Seminar

	**Step 1: Identify specifically how your presentation will support IRACIS.** What resulting improvements in performance will provide more value for the organization than it costs to provide the session? How will that be measured?	From the standpoint of the sponsor, the business case was to decrease the number of sick days (Avoid Costs). The audience of employees was probably thinking of it in different terms; their WIIFM was likely how to manage their time and energy to do more with less. But in a real sense, there was a business case for them too, like avoiding the "cost" of using up their sick days!
	**Step 2: Identify the specific, observable behaviors that will produce that result.** What do happy, healthy, minimal-sick-day-using employees DO in the face of stressful changes? How do they deploy the time, energy and tools at their disposal on the job?	A preliminary list included reducing coffee intake and drinking more water; taking a short walk during lunch; and learning to ask good clarifying questions before responding to a stressful situation.
	**Step 3: Create rehearsal opportunities that use those behaviors.** How might participants practice these things during the session?	• **Individual reflection:** Ask individuals to jot down past occasions when an unwelcome change caused a great deal of stress. What happened? Who was involved? What was the result?

		• **Small group sharing:** Individuals share what they identified with a small number of people. • **Solve real problems:** Exchange a thumbnail description of these past situations (or of a non-work-related current situation) with another group, and have them come up with appropriate coping strategies and share them with the large group. • **Plan future action:** Participants help each other to develop a possible routine to incorporate into their typical work day.
	**Step 4: Identify what participants really, *really* need to know to rehearse successfully.** Now (and only now) you can dig into identifying or/and creating the specific resources participants will need to be successful in the rehearsal opportunities.	In this case you might provide sample scripts that could be used to diffuse the anger of an agitated customer, or details about the Employee Assistance Program offered by the company.

Cut as Much as you Possibly Can, Then Cut a Little Bit More.

It's hard to strip your content to the bare essentials necessary for your learners to succeed at meaningful practice. Those details are important! Who would know that better than you? (Terri and Sheila teach this stuff, and *we* have a hard time pruning all the cool things we want to share.)

Just keep asking yourself questions like these:

- ❑ What if they didn't know that? Could they still get the job done?

- ❑ If push came to shove, could they get by without knowing this?

- ❑ Could they still be effective if they simply knew where to find this information as the need arises?

- ❑ How will giving them that information directly affect our objective?

THE ENGAGING EXPERT

In the spirit of focusing on the "DO" and on rehearsing what you want to do in the Real World, think of a presentation or training you have delivered in the past, and imagine how you could redo it in a way that is explicitly linked to IRACIS.

TOPIC:	
[REVENUE / SERVICE / COSTS figure]	
[DO magnifying glass]	
[Hamlet with skull]	Probably rehearsal opportunities space noticeably larger than the others
[charts icon]	

Prioritize Practice

The impulse to share as much information as possible in the time you have available is understandable. But in the end it is not helpful. Just as you could not have driven by yourself in rush-hour traffic after passing the written portion of a driving test, your learners cannot meaningfully adjust their performance without a chance to practice what you are asking of them.

When you don't provide the rehearsal opportunities in a structured environment rich in feedback, they will in effect be practicing when they get back on the job interacting with colleagues and customers. If it's important that they perform well, help them be successful in the Real World by letting them practice while they are with you.

Remember that room-painting analogy from chapter one? Well, you are finally ready to start putting some metaphorical paint on the walls. And you will find it is considerably easier (and faster) because of the prep work you did.

You're still going to be careful, of course. After all the effort you put into determining whether a presentation was the right tool, figuring out the outcome you are after and how to measure it, identifying the key behaviors and some possible ways to practice them, you're certainly not going to mess it up now by lapsing into the kind of workshop that made you weep with boredom when you were on the receiving end.

In the next section you will find a simple way to structure your session, how to make the pieces fit together smoothly, and techniques for delivering your specific content.

PREPARE TO ENGAGE

"Better attention always equals better learning. We have known for a long time that 'interest' or 'importance' is inextricably linked to attention. ... {Marketing professionals} have known for a long time that novel stimuli — the unusual, unpredictable or distinctive — are powerful ways to harness attention in the service of interest."

—John Medina, Director
Brain Center for Applied Learning Research, Seattle Pacific University

"The more parts of the brain that are engaged when learning something, the better the learning sticks."

—Unknown

Now that you have identified the key concepts and rehearsal opportunities you want to share, you can start to piece them together in a logical sequence.

In this chapter we'll show you how to use a "PIP + close the loop" model to organize the major chunks of your content and how to fit them together smoothly with effective openers, closers and transitions.

We'll also give you plenty of specific techniques (accompanied by worked examples) for delivering your content in ways that minimize passive lectures.

PIP + Close the Loop

This simple formula is a surprisingly robust little tool. It works for your session as a whole as well as for each of the major "chunks" of your content. And you can vary the sequence of the formula from one section to the next.

Present-Illustrate-Practice: For any major "chunk" of your content your audience needs the basic concept (**Present**), examples of how to apply it (**Illustrate**) and time to rehearse applying it themselves (**Practice**).

The beauty of PIP, though, is that it does not have a fixed order. You can start with the illustration, for example, maybe in the form of a vivid anecdote that highlights the consequences of failing to apply a key principle. Or you could jump right into practice; having participants try an activity from which they can deduce the principle you are trying to teach.

The order does not matter. You just need to hit all three for each major element of your content.

Close the Loop: This is where the magic happens. It seems obvious to you, of course, how your content fits into the Real World. *But you cannot assume it will be obvious to your audience.* You need to take them by the figurative hand and walk them through that final connection.

It's not that your participants are any less smart than you. But give them a break! Your content is new to them. And it's not the only thing on their mind. Think of all the things competing for *your* attention at this very moment.

If you are serious about having people apply what you are sharing, then you will not leave this final step to chance.

It need not be an elaborate process. And you can be as direct as simply asking, "How would you apply this back where *you* work?" Or maybe, "How would you have to adjust this to fit your particular circumstances?" Just help your audience make sure they can imagine *doing* what you want them to do.

> ### Your Brain Has a Filter
>
> "Attention, like breathing, tends to be automatically controlled. You can take charge of both for a short time, but as soon as you cease consciously controlling them, they revert to automatic.
>
> "From a training perspective, this is very important. Whether it be a live trainer, a computer learning program or a videotape, *if the learner unconsciously does not feel that the information is vital to his or her needs,* the autonomic system may raise the threshold of sensory input and filter out what is being transmitted." (emphasis added)
>
> Harold Stolovitch & Erica Keeps
Telling Ain't Training

CFU: Check for Understanding

You probably already sprinkle Checks For Understanding (CFUs) throughout your presentation, verifying that your audience understands your content. One way to make a CFU serve two purposes at once is to use it as a way to "close the loop." If your learners can describe how they will apply what they just learned back in their Real World, you can be pretty confident that they grasp what you were trying to teach. And if they don't understand it after all, this is likely to show up in their responses, which will give you an opportunity to clarify concepts that are still fuzzy for your audience.

The following questions are examples that can do double duty as CFUs and a means to "close the loop" after you have finished a PIP cycle on a significant chunk of your content:

- ❏ How will you use this when you get back to your Real World?
- ❏ How can you apply this concept to the work that you do now?
- ❏ How can you administer this new policy (or process) immediately with your staff?
- ❏ What barriers might there be to applying this new policy (or process) with your customers?

> Note that questions like, "Does that make sense?" do not make the list. Anything that solicits a yes-no response is unlikely to give you a clear idea of how much your learners have absorbed. Stick with the classic who-what-where-why-how questions.

Here's an example of PIP + close the loop:

A large professional association radically redesigned its orientation for new members with an eye toward rehearsing behaviors that make the best use of the organization's resources. One of the key behaviors they identified was making deliberate, strategic choices about which of the many participation opportunities to pursue in any given month.

But instead of starting with a straightforward presentation of what the options were, facilitators threw participants straight into **practice**.

On each table were cards describing the different kinds of programming provided by the local chapter and national organization. Pairs of participants got thumbnail profiles of imaginary members with widely divergent circumstances, experience and goals. Their task was to select which chapter offerings they would recommend for each of the imaginary members.

Participants provided the **illustrations** of the target behavior when they shared their recommendations and reasoning with the large group.

The facilitators then **presented** where to find and register for association activities on the website.

Then, to make the connection to the Real World completely unambiguous, participants **closed the loop** by taking a few moments to identify which upcoming events best matched their own goals for their membership.

Here's another example of what PIP + "close the loop" might look like in an outline much like what you might use to plan the flow of your session:

Note that the *methods* for presenting, illustrating, practicing and closing the loop were identified first, and then the *sequence* was determined afterward.

Present	Illustrate	Practice	Close the Loop
What content are you covering? Can you get by with less?	How will you illustrate it?	How will participants "rehearse" applying this content? ①	How will you connect your content to the Real World of your participants?
What participation opportunities are available through the association: • Monthly meetings • Day-long workshops • Special Interest Groups, Etc. ③	Pairs or small groups will report their recommendations to the rest of the group, who can then suggest additional possibilities. ②	Identify appropriate activities to recommend for members with wildly different circumstances; use descriptions of all participation opportunities and thumbnail profiles of imaginary members – different profiles for each pair/small group of participants	Identify upcoming items on calendar that best match their own goals for membership

Since this is a book about learning by *doing*, try identifying a possible PIP + "close the loop" cycle you could use with content you deliver

Present	Illustrate	Practice	Close the Loop
What content are you covering? Can you get by with less?	How will you illustrate it?	How will participants "rehearse" applying this content?	How will you connect your content to the Real World of your participants?

Bookend Your Content

To give each cycle of PIP + "close the loop" and, indeed, your entire presentation the most sticking power, think carefully about your beginnings and endings. Craft your openers, closers and transitions well, and you increase the sticking power of your message substantially.

Primacy-Recency Effect

During a learning event, we remember best whatever came first. We remember second best what came last. We remember least what came in the middle. (We also tend to assume that items at the beginning and end are of greater importance.)

One reason for the Primacy Effect is that the listener's brain is busy processing the initial information. This makes that "middle" time ideal for practicing and engaging learners more deeply in the new material you just presented.

Veteran educator John Cafarella of www.sciencegnus.com illustrates the idea this way: (Reprinted with permission.)

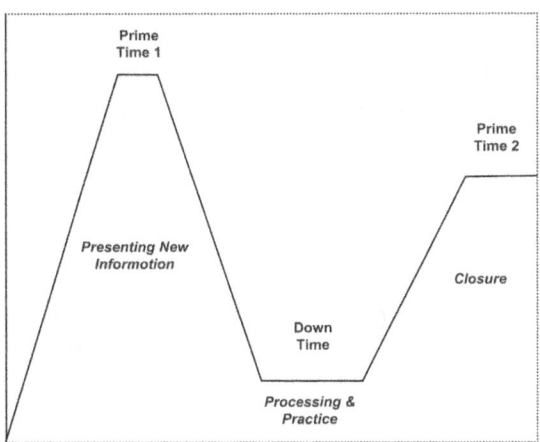

You may be familiar with Primacy-Recency Effect. People tend to remember the last part of what they heard better than any other part of a sequence. And they remember the first part better than the middle.

Given this, why would you want to waste "prime real estate" of beginnings and endings for your material on anything that does not directly support the outcome you want from the session? This is particularly important about your session as a whole, but it also applies to the major sections of your content.

Yet presenters squander this precious time with alarming regularity. For example, how many times have you deliberately arrived just a bit late to a workshop so you could avoid the silly "ice breaker" that kicks off so many training sessions? (Or maybe you just wished you had arrived late.)

Not that breaking the proverbial ice is not important. Groups that learn each others' names and interact right away are generally ready to learn sooner than those that don't.

If you AIIM your openers, though, you can use the Primacy Effect to launch directly into your topic *and* to warm up the group.

Openers

A powerful opener gets participants' **Attention**. It encourages **Immediate Interaction** with each other. And its focus is **Meaningful**, as in directly pertaining to your content.

That is what distinguishes openers from "ice breakers," which too often resemble the sorts of games you might find at a baby shower or similar party.

Attention: Most of us are pretty preoccupied with our own stuff, and it can take a while for us to switch our full attention to a presentation, particularly if it starts off slow. A good opener provides a compelling reason to pay attention right away.

Immediate Interaction: Newly formed groups (even when at least some of the members already know each other) have a certain level of awkwardness and even anxiety until they feel out what will be the "norms" of the particular group in the particular context. Providing a structured way to interact speeds up the process of establishing comfortable norms and frees up more attention for learning.

Meaningful: Anything you include in your workshop should relate unambiguously to your content and your intended outcome. Anything else will justifiably be considered a waste of time – a precious resource in our fast-paced culture.

How much time should an opener take?

2-hour session ...... 3-5 min

Half-day session .....10 min

Full-day session ......15 min

Value-Added Introductions

Formal introductions can serve as an opener, particularly when you use them to gather more information about your audience and their objectives.

It is common to have participants give their name, formal position, and organization or department. Sometimes facilitators add something intended as fun to this list, like the most recent movie the person saw. Why not make this something purposeful, like years of experience in the field or their primary objective for attending?

Large-Group Adaptation: You can still include introductions when you have a very large group. Have people introduce themselves to successive partners or to sub-groups. Then ask volunteers or table representatives to summarize the information they heard. This takes advantage of the way audiences warm up faster when they get to interact, and it still allows you to collect useful information without eating into too much of your presentation time.

Sample Openers

Flag the Handouts: Prime participants for your content by giving them a few minutes to page through the handouts and flag (with sticky notes or a marker) one to three things that make them curious or that they might be particularly interested in. Then have them share what they marked with a partner or table mates (or, if your audience is small, with the whole group).

Gallery Walk: Another way to prime participants for your content is to have pairs or small groups walk around the room looking at visual aids you have posted and discuss what each might mean. You can build curiosity by deliberately making these visual aids so they won't make much sense until you cover the related content.

Human Scramble: Have participants share something specific with successive partners. For example, ask them to write down one or two things they hope to get out of the training or that they plan to DO with what they learn. Give pairs a minute or so to talk before signaling that they should switch partners. People will probably refine their own objectives as they hear those of others, and this is a good thing. At the end ask for a few volunteers to share their (likely refined) objectives for the session with the large group. Or have people write them on sticky notes and post them at the front of the room, which allows others (including you) to review them.

Buddy Charts: Have participants find a partner. Give each pair a piece of flip-chart paper to post on the wall and markers. In one column each have partner A record the responses of partner B to some get-acquainted questions you provide (e.g., name, company, objectives for being here, etc.). Then B does the same for A.

> **Re-purpose this:** Throughout your session as modules are completed, have partners meet at their chart and write down one or two things they learned and what they will do as a result. The movement makes it an energizer, and what they write down serves as a review and a way to "close the loop" to the Real World.

Transitions

When you do them well, your audience probably won't even notice good transitions from one section of your content to the next. But they will notice their absence.

Ideally a transition is only a few sentences long. It neatly ties up the content you are closing and makes clear the connection between that and the new material you are about to introduce.

Crafting clean, transparent transitions can go a long way toward both adding polish to your session and, interestingly enough, calming your own jitters.

> ### Sample Transitions
>
> - "Take a minute to jot a few notes on your action plan before we move to the next section. Then we'll dive into how this particular way of tracking your

> activity will make it much simpler to comply with the new regulation."
>
> - "Now that you have a good grasp of why the conditions have changed so radically in our industry, let's take a look at how we can exploit the opportunity this opens up for us."
>
> - "My co-facilitator taught us to manipulate the new equipment with ease. Let's spend some time confirming next steps in getting everyone else on board."
>
> - "Just as my co-facilitator indicated, the market is slow to recover here, and this means…."

When you are co-presenting with other people, practice your hand-offs – or at least talk through exactly how you are going to do them. You wouldn't want to have the impact of your carefully crafted closer or opener inadvertently undermined with a competing, redundant or awkward hand-off. On the other hand, smooth hand-offs can make mediocre openers and closers appear more polished than they otherwise would.

> ### Earn Their Attention Again
>
> In his book *Brain Rules: 12 Principles for Surviving and Thriving at Work, Home, and School*, John Medina writes, "Peer-reviewed studies confirm my informal inquiry: Before the first quarter hour is over in a typical presentation, people *usually* have

checked out. If keeping someone's interest in a lecture were a business, it would have an 80 percent failure rate."

All is not lost, however. Medina continues, "Audiences check out after 10 minutes, but you can keep grabbing them back by telling narratives or creating events rich in emotion."

How do you trigger an emotion, such as fear, laughter, nostalgia or incredulity in your audience when you transition between blocks of content? Here are a few examples:

- Use a startling statistic or assertion about your subject

- Tell a quick story related to your subject

- Make a vivid, concrete comparison of a key concept to something they can relate to (for example, help them grasp extraordinary volume by explaining how many Olympic-sized swimming pools something would fill)

- Pose a thought-provoking question about your subject

Notice that every single one of these examples includes the idea of making your emotional "hook" explicitly relevant to your content. Simply cracking a joke or sharing some unrelated anecdote will make your presentation seem disjointed.

Closers

"Oh, look! We're out of time. Be sure to complete an evaluation on your way out."

Think about what that does to the energy in a room. And think about the squandered opportunity to apply the Recency Rule to reinforce what you want people to DO with what they learned after they leave.

But closers are not just for the end of your session. One of the secrets to helping participants learn is to review early and often. Purposeful closers, then, should happen in some form after every major chunk of content (and before breaks), not just as your whole session comes to a close.

But we strongly recommend avoiding the engagement-killing phrase, "Let's review." It tends to be a cue for brains to think, "Been there. Done that. What's for lunch, anyway?" Good presenters do lots of reviews, but they avoid using the R-word.

Why Wait?

If you are using evaluation forms, they don't have to wait for the very end. Try having participants complete their "smile sheets" three-quarters of the way through your presentation. Not only does this leave you time for a powerful close, but you are likely to get much more thoughtful comments.

Tip: To make sure you get them back, you can use completed evaluation forms as "tickets" for a drawing of some kind at the end of the session.

"Reboot" After Breaks

After people have been away from your content for a while, they need some time to switch their attention back to where you need it to be. This is especially true if you have multiple sessions separated by hours or days. But it also holds true after a brief coffee or lunch break. Take a moment to help them refocus on what they have already learned so you can build on it more quickly.

Sample Closers

"Why" Cards: Identify major concepts from your session, and write each one on a 3x5 card in the form of a "why" question. For example, "Why would presenters want to avoid saying, 'Let's review'?" Have participants draw cards randomly in their small groups or pairs, and share their own responses.

"Cheat" Cards: Distribute three 3x5 cards to each participant. Have them create "cheat sheets" they can post in their work area to help them apply what they learned back in the Real World.

Random Sharing: On a single sheet of paper have participants write their answer(s) to one or more questions along the lines of the following: What is the most important concept we covered today? What was the most useful thing you learned today? Identify three specific things you will DO as a result of what you learned here today. Randomly redistribute the papers so no one has their own, then have participants read the one they happen to end up with to the rest of the group. (To add energy to this process, gather the group in a circle to read aloud what they have. The movement and the novelty alert the brain that something worth attending to is going on.)

Random Redistribution - the easy way: Ask designated participants to collect all the answer pages, shuffle them, and hand them out again randomly.

Random Redistribution - a bit more fun: Gather participants in a cluster. Have them fold their answer pages into quarters, and have them continually trade the folded papers randomly with other participants for as long as there is music playing. When the music stops, each person shares with the group the responses he or she happens to be holding.

Random Redistribution - for high-energy groups: Have participants fold their own answer page into a paper airplane (or crumple them into a "snowball"). Initiate an "all-fly zone" (or a "snowball fight") for as long as there is music playing. When the music stops, each person retrieves the page closest to him or her, unfolds (or uncrumples) it, and shares the responses with the group.

More high-energy randomness: Try having participants write their response(s) on balloons they blow up. While music plays, participants toss balloons around, trying to keep them all in the air at the same time. When the music stops, participants read to the group whatever is on the balloon closest to them.

> **Add Polish the Easy Way**
>
> If you are able to practice only one or two elements of your presentation, practice your opening, your closing and your transitions. These are the points where your momentum and concentration are most vulnerable. Knowing you can deliver these elements with confidence does a lot to put you at ease. This in turn frees up mental resources to focus on your message and your audience rather than your nerves.

Interaction Matters

Deliberately promoting interaction among participants helps them learn. Some estimates claim that people learn as much from each other (or even more from each other) as from the facilitator.

That's not an entirely unreasonable claim. The collective knowledge in the room may, in fact, equal or surpass that of the presenter alone. Terri and Sheila have a combined 58 years of formal experience teaching others. But when we speak to groups of peers, the combined experience in the room can be many times that.

Whether or not your audience has extensive knowledge of your topic, encouraging deliberate interaction among your learners – in ways that engage them with your content – will help them retain what you are trying to teach them.

Alternatives to Lecture

You don't have to be "that presenter." The one who drones on and on . . . and on . . . and on. Even when you are called in at the last minute, or asked to deliver someone else's material, or assigned a "canned" presentation that gives you little leeway, there are plenty of ways to keep your audience alert and engaged. We'll start with the simplest and work our way to the most active.

You might notice that we are using basically a PIP + "close the loop" model throughout this section. We *Present* the technique; then we *Illustrate* it with examples that we hope will help you imagine how you might adapt the technique to your own circumstances. While providing *Practice* in a book form is something of a challenge, we do offer some hints and questions for you to think about, again with the intent of helping you *close the loop* on how you will apply the ideas in your Real World.

Use a Story

If you sincerely believe you have no practical way to avoid an information dump, you can dramatically increase its staying power by sharing it in the form of a story.

Human beings are wired for stories. Stories provide context for dry material or abstractions. (In fact, the examples in this chapter are in effect stories that show the contextual application of the abstract descriptions of the techniques.) And stories have a way of demonstrating the WIIFM (What's In It For Me?) in a way few other techniques can match.

Managing Money Not Their Own

A non-profit organization was feeling the consequences of providing inadequate resources to guide volunteers who handled money on its behalf. The finance director identified several principles volunteers would need to implement to get the target result of avoiding messy disputes, wildly insufficient documentation for the IRS, and the occasional lawsuit.

Most volunteers were already aware of the fact that they should save receipts, code their expenses and keep clear records. But they didn't really know the steps involved in doing that. And besides that, they were sure that whatever the process was supposed to be, it was too complicated and cumbersome to be worth the bother. They were volunteers, after all.

The facilitators had half an hour with most groups of volunteers. And in those 30 minutes they had to cover lots of rules and forms and, of course, they had to persuade a semi-hostile audience to change their behavior significantly.

So the training became the story of a year in the life of Joe Volunteer. Joe was a lot like most of the audience. He had a full-time job and a family, and he volunteered for the organization because he loved the interaction with people.

The story started with Joe's resolution to avoid the snafus of how he tracked the money for which he was responsible the previous year. The handouts were the completed forms Joe Volunteer used at each step in the process, along with samples of how Joe maintained the checkbook and kept track of his receipts. All the examples reflected the details of Joe's specific story.

"Last year Joe just threw all his receipts in an envelope, which was way better than not collecting them at all. But he'd had a devil of a time trying to reconstruct what all the receipts were for when he completed his year-end report. It took hours! So this year he simply added a note and a code whenever he 'filed' a receipt in his envelope."

The 30-minute money-tracking presentation became a hit among volunteers, who immediately adopted many of the suggestions directly from the session. The story was, after all, about making Joe's life easier, not more complicated.

Interestingly, one of the facilitators was not quite sold on the whole story idea, and when her time was shortened to 20 minutes with one group, she skipped it. She only shared the handouts and told her audience of volunteers the rules for documenting how money flowed through the organization. In the end it actually took her more than 30 minutes, since she had to field so many questions. The evaluations reflected how unhappy the volunteers were with the presentation, and very few of them made significant changes to their documentation habits.

Compelling Case for Airline Safety

Some unfortunate incidents made an airline aware that fight attendants were frequently flying without their bulky checklist books. These books spelled out, among other things, pre-flight routines for a variety of aircraft. The veteran flight attendants figured they had the important stuff memorized, and the new people didn't want to stand out as novices.

Alarmed, the airline mandated training for all flight attendants on the importance of using their checklist books at the start of each and every flight. (How would you like to be designing the presentation for *that* audience?)

Rather than start with a list of learning objectives or a defensive justification for holding the training in the first place, the session started off with a short video clip. The first image was of an airplane in distress over water. Dramatic music played over radio voices issuing a mayday call for help. The frantic music continued as the view switched to the inside of the cabin from the perspective of a flight attendant speeding down the aisle. In her voiceover she was mentally running through the preflight checklist, assuring herself that she had in fact checked each item. Then the camera zoomed in on a gauge she saw as she arrived at the rear exit of the plane and reached to deploy the chute. "Oh, no!" she cried. "There's no pressure!"

Then the screen went black.

String Them Along

This is actually a variation on storytelling. Why provide an answer when you can start with a question? Mysteries are powerful, creating a need for closure. This technique lends itself particularly well to sharing complex information. Introduce your mystery at the start of your presentation, return to it during your presentation, and wait to reveal the answer at the end.

> ### Mystery of the Rings
>
> In their book *Made to Stick: Why Some Ideas Survive and Others Die*, Chip Heath and Dan Heath describe a science lecture that held students' rapt attention right to the end. Instead of simply explaining what the rings of Saturn are made of, the professor framed it as a mystery. Three internationally acclaimed groups of scientists trying to identify the make-up of the Saturn rings had come to three very different conclusions. How could that be? Who was right?
>
> Students' curiosity and need to know the answer deepened as the astronomer described the methods of following up promising leads and the heartbreak of dead ends as each team of scientists tested its theory.
>
> Even with just these few sentences of description, are *you* curious about what the rings of Saturn are made of? Imagine the effect on your audience if you were describing the vivid, humanizing details of *your* topic framed as a mystery at the beginning of your session. (The answer to the mystery of the rings, by the way, turned out to be ice-covered dust. Who knew dust could be so engaging?)

Jarring Start

"I'll explain some new ways for you to accomplish your objectives," the speaker said. "Then I'll explain why you will fail."

Huh? The speech was supposed to be inspirational, part of a change-management initiative that aimed to alter the very culture of the company. Why would the speaker start with a promise of failure? Was it a rebuke? A challenge? An effort to reassure?

The lingering questions changed how the audience listened to the presentation. How would the speaker resolve the tension created in the introduction?

By the time the "failure" part of the speech came around, the context had been established. There was no sugar-coating the difficulties ahead; they would be uncomfortable. There was an unavoidable element of trial and error, since the situation was entirely new to everyone involved. "You will have bad days," the speaker said. "But you can turn bad days into good data. Here's how."

Get Ongoing Feedback

People will listen differently to presentations when they are asked to signal their understanding periodically.

Sample Ways to Solicit Feedback

- **A-B-C Cards:** Provide participants large cards with the letters A, B, C, D – one letter per card. (You could also have participants make these themselves.) Periodically during your presentation, pose a multiple-choice question, and instead of singling out one person to respond, have everyone hold up the card corresponding with what they think is the right answer.

    Tip: Give participants a way to signal, "I don't have any idea what the answer is." For example, have them display the A card sideways or upside down.

- **Green-Yellow-Red Cards:** Provide participants with one card of each color, and ask them to keep them where you can easily see one of the colors at all times. If they are following what you are saying, they should display the green card. If they are getting lost, display the yellow. If they find themselves disagreeing with or objecting to what you are saying, display the red.

- **Muddiest Point:** At the start of your presentation ask participants to write down the "muddiest point" as you go along. Part way through the session, collect the responses and call a break to allow you to review them and determine how to address them when the break is over.

Assign Questions

Yes, literally assign specific, random individuals to ask a question (one that you have provided in advance or one that the individual generates on the spot) at a specific time. To add some suspense or a game-like element, set a timer to go off randomly to indicate that it is time for the next person's question. This increases audience participation, makes them keep focus, *and* allows them to ask for clarification.

Find the Question

A speaker from the Medical Director's office was invited to address call-center employees at a medical insurance company to help them understand the impact of their assistance to patients.

Taped under each chair were pieces of paper that had either an answer or a question pertaining to services delivered during the past year. As part of the warm-up for her presentation, the speaker asked for a volunteer with a question to read it to the group. Then anyone who thought they had the corresponding answer in their hand was to offer that to the group.

Some of the questions were pretty straightforward. The person holding the paper saying "just over 1,200" had no trouble identifying it as the answer to "How many employees are currently providing services to our patients?" The exchange provided the opening for the speaker to describe how patients were served in the hospitals, clinics, home-health sites, etc.

> Other connections were not so obvious. When multiple people thought they might be holding the right answer, a rich discussion ensued. The format kept the entire audience engaged (and even amazed) for the whole exercise.

> ### Warming Up a Shy Group
>
> A world-renowned specialist in information management systems was invited to address French-speaking graduate students at the Institut de Gestion (School of Business) of the Université de Rennes in France. His presentation would be in English.
>
> Knowing that the students would be shy about speaking up in a foreign language – particularly *during* a lecture from an invited guest instead of at the end – he randomly picked out several individuals in the audience at the beginning of his talk.
>
> "You there in the pink sweater. Yes, you, my dear. When I give you the signal, I want you to ask me a question. I don't care what it is. If you can't think of anything, just ask me about the weather or something. I simply want you to ask the first question."
>
> The students were mortified initially, of course. But despite some stammering and a couple of off-topic questions, the group warmed up to this alien way of doing things. By the afternoon of the daylong seminar, hands were going up spontaneously, and the expert was gleefully fielding excellent questions as they arose.

Generate Questions for Others

Have participants generate questions for their fellow learners on key ideas as you go along. This changes how learners listen to the content of your message, since it requires more engagement (more of the brain!) to evaluate the relative importance of the ideas and articulate them in a form clear to others.

You can collect the questions to use as the basis for a review activity. You could even make it a game, awarding points to teams for correct answers.

Capturing Key Ideas for Others . . . Times Two

During a session on employment law, the instructor asked participants to use the individual index cards on their tables to jot down key ideas, phrases or terms that they heard in the session, one idea per notecard.

At the end of the session the notes were collected, shuffled and redistributed to all participants. Each person selected what they considered to be the best note in their hand (another round of comparing ideas and assessing their relative importance) to read aloud and explain to the rest of the group. In effect, the learners participated actively in the delivery of what would otherwise have been passive lecture.

To "reboot" the topic after the lunch break, the facilitator asked participants to craft three test questions that anyone present during the morning session should be able to answer. The questions were left on the tables where the small groups were seated. Then learners went to different tables (movement) in newly scrambled small groups to answer the questions they found there.

Count Your Words

When you put an arbitrary constraint on how many words participants must use to express key ideas, you make them prioritize concepts and express them in their own words. This, again, demands a whole lot more processing power from their brains than listening alone or even taking notes.

The Incredible Shrinking Summary

Ask participants (as individuals, pairs or small groups) to craft a summary of key ideas that is a specific number of words long — say, no more than 37 words and no fewer than 31. Ask for volunteers to share what they wrote with the large group.

Then ask learners to do the same thing in fewer words — say, no more than 28 and no fewer than 23. Again ask volunteers to share.

Keep repeating the process with fewer and fewer words. For fun you could extend it to the point of ridiculous: No more than two words, for example.

This activity produces a surprising amount of energy and usually laughter as participants compete to come up with the best summary in tighter and tighter constraints. It is also fairly demanding, requiring learners to compare and rephrase concepts, which uses a whole lot more brain power than simply listening or even taking notes. And of course, participants are hearing key concepts repeatedly and in a variety of forms from a variety of people — another way to help them retain what they learn.

Tweet It!

Ask participants to express key concepts as something they could post on Twitter, which allows no more than 140 characters per tweet.

For example: *Providing structured practice time in class makes learning meaningful for the Real World, where measurable business results really matter!*

For much of your audience this will be a familiar exercise, but it still demands a deeper understanding of the material than using an unlimited number of words.

Find the Error

Inform learners at the beginning of your presentation (or of a specific section of your presentation) that there will be one error in your material. Clearly this works best for people already familiar with your topic. How obvious or subtle you make the error depends on the level of expertise of your audience.

A Natural High

In an article from "strategy+business" [sic], a Booz Allen Hamilton magazine, executives seeking to refocus their organizations are advised to study breakthroughs in brain research.

Among the relevant findings: The brain pushes back when told what to do. This is attributed to homeostasis, the movement of organisms toward equilibrium and away from change.

> On the other hand, brains will release an adrenaline-like rush of neurotransmitters when people figure out how to solve a problem themselves rather than being told how to solve it by highers-up.

Walk the Gallery

Put posters or other materials on the walls around the room. Then have pairs or small groups walk from one item to the next, (Movement! And it's purposeful and relevant!) answering specific questions about the materials. This technique can make an excellent opener or closer.

"Rebooting" After Lunch

A favorite of Terri and Sheila is to use a gallery walk after lunch in a day-long workshop. The posters we use as visual aids deliberately do not have many words on them, so they are somewhat puzzling until the content has been covered in the session. (An element of mystery.)

To regain participants' attention and to help them switch mental gears back to the topic, we have pairs or small groups rotate around the room, taking turns explaining to each other what each poster means and how to apply the principle it illustrates.

The movement helps with the post-lunch "food coma," as does the low-key way of getting all of the learners actively engaged at once.

Brainstorm on Your Feet

Try this variation on a classic. Post questions or topics on flip-chart paper around the perimeter of the room. Participants (individuals, pairs or small groups) armed with markers write their answers directly on the flip-chart pages and then move on to the next one, where they add to what was already written there by the previous group(s).

To finish this, have participants rotate through a second time to see what everyone else wrote. Better yet, help them think through the answers more thoroughly by having them rank their top two or three favorite responses on each page. (Comparisons require more brain power – more "hooks" for content to cling to.)

Milk this one a little bit further by tallying up the most popular responses and have participants explain what makes these the best.

Imaginary Customers

During their initial training, new employees at a large co-op did a walking brainstorming session to identify as many ways as possible that the co-op could serve specific kinds of member-customers. Flip-chart pages around the room described specific circumstances of a representative "typical" member-customer, and small clusters of participants wrote down what they could do for each one. Since the new employees came from all parts of the company, they brought richly varied perspectives to the task. During the second walk-through participants got a powerful sense of how all the different departments contributed to the experience of their member-customers and how the efforts of each department could affect the others.

Reverse Roles with a Teach-Back

Turn your learners into teachers. This can work extremely well when you have a large chunk of content to present and the temptation is strong to launch into a long lecture. Instead, provide pairs or small groups with short portions of the content you want them to learn about, a different part for each group. Then give the groups time to read through the material and pick out the key ideas most useful to the rest of the people who happen to be in the session. (This means comparing and prioritizing concepts for real people in the Real World.) Then, you guessed it! Have *them* present that content to the large group.

This offers a change of pace for participants, since they are getting the content from different people besides you. And somehow seeing your fellow learners do the teaching tends to make the materials a bit more interesting than it would otherwise be. Best of all, most of the time you will be pleasantly surprised with the creativity and impact of the presentations.

> ### Even By-laws Can Be Interesting
>
> Board members are presumed to be familiar with the policies and by-laws of their organization. But how do you make sure everyone has at least a passing familiarity with those devastatingly dry pages and their implications?
>
> At their annual planning retreat one year, board members for a professional association were paired up and assigned a few specific pages of the by-laws. Their task was to pick out the most critical concepts on those particular pages, explain them to the rest of the group, and give an example of their implications in the regular operation of the association.

> They were encouraged to use stories and anecdotes to illustrate their points, and in under an hour those dry pages of legal language became more "real" than they had ever been before.

Do Role Plays for Everyone at Once

The words "role play" can strike terror into the hearts of learners everywhere, since they tend to imagine two or more hapless "volunteers" acting out a scene in front of the whole group. But you can make much more effective use of the technique by having lots of them going on at once, which is much less daunting to most participants. Get everyone actively engaged in purposeful activity at the same time in small groups or pairs.

> ### Practicing by Threes
>
> In a coaching-skills session for supervisors, threesomes were given brief descriptions of situations requiring corrective feedback to an employee. One person played the supervisor, of course, and another the employee. The third person did not get to see the scenario in advance. That person's role was to listen to the interaction. Afterwards, he or she described what she heard and provided specific feedback to the other two. Then the triads rotated roles and went on to a new scenario.

Uncovering Hidden Information

In a project-management workshop for accountants, role players in pairs each received a different version of the same situation – one from the perspective of the project lead (the In-Charge, in the language of the accounting firm), and the other from the perspective of a team member (Staff Person) on the project. Each participant had information that the other did not, and their task was to surface all the facts they needed and determine a course of action.

Situation: A staff person is not requesting guidance at appropriate times, and the In-Charge has done insufficient follow-up on the work delegated to this person.

In-Charge: Louise

- You are nearing the end of an Engagement with Darrell.

- It was just the two of you on this Engagement, which was a bit trying. Darrell seems to think the two of you should be buddies or something. He's always talking about his weekend plans and such instead of just getting the work done.

- Darrell has been with the Firm for over three years, so he should know what he is doing by now. But you often find he lacks attention to detail, and he seems to want a lot of handholding when he should be looking things up for himself.

- You are anxious to just get this Engagement over with and move on.

- You just discovered that the accrual for self-insurance that you delegated to Darrell was done wrong, and now the two of you will have to do a great deal of re-work to fix it.

- It is so frustrating that Darrell doesn't seem to understand when to do things himself and when to ask for help – and to ask for it in a direct, specific way.

Situation: A staff person is not requesting guidance at appropriate times, and the In-Charge has done insufficient follow-up on the work delegated to this person.

Staff Person: Darrell

- You are nearing the end of an Engagement with Louise.

- It was just the two of you on this Engagement, which was a bit trying. Louise is so unsociable and blunt. She seems to have the empathy of a lawn mower.

- Normally you can charm people like this into a relatively good relationship, but Louise is just too spiky. You have essentially resigned yourself to surviving the Engagement. In the meantime you try to avoid contact with Louise when possible.

- Now Louise is upset because you did something wrong on the accrual for self insurance, which will require a great deal of re-work.

- You had tried to ask her about it as you were doing it, but she seemed to think you were whining or something. So you tried to find your answers on your own and muddle through.

Deduce the Abstract from the Concrete

When learners are trying to internalize new content, particularly abstract content, it's not going to have much sticking power without plenty of concrete examples. To accelerate this process, why not start with the examples and have your learners use them to figure out the abstraction for themselves?

> ### What Rules Do You See?
>
> This example is from information architect and behavioral scientist Chris Atherton. She used two different ways to present the formatting rules for Harvard referencing. Guess which one resulted in better understanding and retention.
>
> Here's one way of teaching Harvard referencing:
>
> * Surname followed by initials
>
> * Year of publication
>
> * Title of article
>
> * Title of journal (italics), its volume (italics), page numbers.

> Here's a different way of teaching referencing:
>
> *What are the rules by which this reference list is organized? Name as many as you can.*
>
> Aardvark, J.R. (1980). Ants, and how to eat them. *Journal of Orycteropodidae Studies, 80,* 11-17.
>
> Barker, R. (1982). *Rum babas, and what to do if you've got them.* Reading: Goodnight From Him.
>
> Halley, W. (1955) *Rock Around The Clock.* New York: Decca.
>
> Izzard, E. (1998) Cake or Death? *Gateaunomics, 10,* 195-196.
>
> Lemur, R.-T. (2010) *Strepsirrhinoplasty.* Antananarivo: Raft Press.
>
> Leonard, E. (1996). *Out of Sight.* New York: Harper.
>
> Shorty, G. (in press). *Okay, so they got me.* Los Angeles: Cadillac.

Take a Practice Test

An awful lot of new research suggests that using tests as learning tools is noticeably more effective than studying or review alone – particularly when practice tests are accompanied by meaningful feedback.

The key is to practice retrieving the new knowledge from memory, which is what learners will have to do in the Real World.

According to *The Princeton Review,*

> Practice tests are far more helpful than repeatedly reading the material or even making outlines or concept maps. Those other strategies can lead you to believe that you know the information better than you actually do. In one study, students who used those techniques retrieved only 2/3 of the information that was retrieved by students who used practice tests to study (even though they had greater confidence that they would do well on the test).

The Testing Effect

Essentially, recent experiments in the field of cognitive psychology have shown that learners who practice active recall of information during their study sessions by testing or quizzing themselves on the learning content are able to recall more information on the actual exam and receive higher scores. Termed the "testing effect, this methodology highlights how frequent memory retrieval strengthens the connections between the synapses of the original memory and as a result, the recall-ability of a memory becomes easier in some instances learners have been able to recall 300% more information!

(from "The Testing Effect" whitepaper by Knowledge Factor)

Don't forget that simply demonstrating that they can perform a skill is itself a very effective test of whether participants have learned your material – particularly with procedural knowledge that people can often "do" but cannot put into words.

Learning to Survive a Chemical Attack

In basic training, new army recruits have a strong incentive to learn to put on, clear and seal a gas mask quickly. After practicing the skill several times, they test their proficiency in a gas chamber in which a cyanide-based (but non-lethal) gas is released. "That stuff makes tear gas seem like Chanel No. 5!" said one trainee.

This skill is reinforced throughout the rest of basic training; at any moment a drill sergeant can sound the chemical-alarm signal, and trainees must stop whatever they are doing and mask up in less than nine seconds.

Instant Testing

Ask participants to create a three- or four-question test about your material. Have them write it out by hand on a single piece of paper, leaving room for someone else to write in the answers.

Collect all the tests, and redistribute them randomly. Give participants a few minutes to write in their answers. Then ask each person to choose one question and their answer to share with the rest of the group. Or have the person share just the question and ask for volunteers in the large group to give the answer.

Play a Game

We held this one for last because it's often trickier than you might think to make games serve as genuinely relevant rehearsal opportunities. When was the last time your boss asked you to frame your response in the form of a question?

For that matter, when was the last time a colleague or customer asked you to provide a definition for a specific term or choose one of four multiple-choice options? More likely they want your help to solve a problem.

The key to making games into rehearsal opportunities is to make sure that your scoring system is based on some decision-making or other behavior that reflects what learners will DO back in the Real World.

Learning to Stay Thin in a Restaurant

A hospital's weight-management class included a session on making weight-conscious choices in restaurants, including fast-food restaurants.

After a presentation on key principles to apply, participants got to "order" at several "restaurants" in the room. Under a sign with the name of a real restaurant were cutout images of real items from their actual menu. Participants selected items they thought would keep their total intake of calories, fat or carbohydrates below a certain target.

Once their "order" at a given restaurant was complete, participants could flip over the images to see the actual calories, fat or carbohydrates they would have consumed. Winners were the ones whose total intake was closest to the total of all the targets.

One Topic, Many Methods

Below is a smattering of examples of different ways to present the very same content, in this case how to identify actionable harassment in the workplace.

- **Video** of conversations in a workplace. Ask partners or small groups to address the following questions:
    - Is harassment present in this situation? What makes you think so?
    - What additional information do you need to make that determination?
    - If appropriate, what would be a "respectful" response on your part?
    - What should management do about it?

  Debrief by asking for a report from one group and then additional responses from others. Be clear about the legal interpretation.
- **Written scenarios** of the same sorts of conversations. Again, ask partners or small groups to address the same questions as above, and debrief in the same way.
- **Guided storytelling** using "scripts" of interactions written on individual numbered slips of paper placed randomly under participants' chairs or taped to the back of their participant guides. Debrief in the large group with the same questions.
- **Walking brainstorming** using several scenarios on large posters scattered around the room, followed by one or more of the above questions. Provide markers to pairs or small groups to write their responses and then continue to the next poster and add to what is already written there. Debrief by discussing agreements and differences in responses.
- **Stand if this is you** activity. Everyone begins from the standing position. As the facilitator (or a volunteer!) reads each of a series of statements aloud, participants sit and then immediately stand back up if the statement applies to them. If it doesn't apply, they remain standing. Example statements:
    - I am aware that there are many types of workplace harassment.
    - I have joined in the conversation when I heard a colleague complain about another's religious customs.
    - I avoid telling off-color jokes in the workplace.
- **Vote with your feet** activity. Have participants stand and go to either the side of the room designated "harmful" or "harmless" to indicate their responses to a series of thumbnail scenarios.

Now that you have planned an impactful, engaging session packed with rehearsal opportunities, you are ready to create the handouts, PowerPoint slides and other visual aids that will support your message.

A few adjustments in your approach can magnify their impact dramatically.

SUPPORT YOUR MESSAGE

PowerPoint is the only form of torture still legal in the United States. But I believe PowerPoint can be used for good. I believe that one day no one will read their slides aloud to an audience that has already read them in their head. I believe that one day presenters will check their figures before they present them. I believe that one day people from HR will join hands with people from engineering and say, "I understood why we had to sit through that!"

—Tim Lee, *biologist turned stand-up comedian*

The trick to making your supporting materials impactful is to remember their *supporting* role. Their whole purpose is to help your learners absorb what you are trying to teach them.

So your top priority is to make them useful during your session. Not that you won't provide reference materials for later use if it is appropriate. But if you are going to use handouts, PowerPoint and other visual aids during your presentation, make sure they enhance your session and work *with* your participants' brains as an aid to learning.

Then you can tweak your post-session materials such as job aids and references to increase the chances that your learners will actually use them back in the Real World.

> ### Serve Your Audience
>
> "Place a greater emphasis on serving the audience instead of delivering the content, and you will discover that your approach to the presentation will change.
>
> "You will want to have a conversation instead of a content dump. To start a conversation, all you need is a persuasive visual that contains a summary headline and a visual that illustrates your point.
>
> "This is your starting point to then explain what is behind the visual, tell a story that illustrates the point further, or engage the audience in thinking about the point. You will get rid of the overloaded text slides that constrain you in your presentation."
>
> David Paradi
author of *The Visual Slide Revolution*

High-Impact Improvements to PowerPoint Slides

PowerPoint is an expected fact of life in many, if not most, contexts in which an expert is called upon to share with a group. We prefer not to rely on PowerPoint for every aspect of a presentation, but many experts do. So you may as well wring the greatest possible benefit from the tool.

PowerPoint sometimes gets a bad rap, which is a pity, really, since it can be a very effective aid.

Simply remember that *you* **are the show, not your slides**.

Your audience is there to see *you* and learn from your expertise. Your slides are there to help you communicate your message.

What if the projector suddenly died before you had a chance to read or explain a slide? How would you illustrate your point?

Now start with *that* idea and build a slide that supports it.

How would you illustrate your point in a conversation? You would only capture the most critical elements of your idea to help the other people understand what you were saying.

What follows are a few pointers that will help you transform typical slides into powerful supports for your message. Essentially they all boil down to the same over-arching theme: **Make your meaning clear at a glance.**

How do you do that? Whole books are devoted to the topic of making the meaning of your slides clear at a glance. For people looking for just a few high-impact pointers, we recommend two tactics:

Use three elements for every slide: headline + severely limited text + graphic element.

Illustrate, don't decorate: Any graphic element on a slide should help viewers grasp the key idea of the slide.

Use Three Elements for Every Slide

Avoid using the built-in templates, which tend to favor bullet-point lists. This may encourage you to put fewer words on the screen, but it does little to enhance your message, let alone make your slides more effective.

On the other hand, if you abandon the templates, how are you supposed to organize the content of your slides?

Fear not! You are not alone in a design wilderness. If you use the three elements we recommend as your "default" slide design, positioning them should occur pretty naturally.

A clear headline

Minimal text necessary

A graphic element

Headline: A clear headline should show unambiguously the conclusion you want the audience to draw from the slide. Don't make your audience dig for the meaning you are trying to convey. They have plenty on their minds already, not least of which is paying attention to what you are saying. Have mercy on their poor, multi-tasking brains, if for no other reason than to give your message more sticking power.

Text: It is trendy in some circles to banish text from slides altogether. But research shows that the most powerful tactic is to use a combination of (very limited) text and images. Use the absolute minimum number of words you need to make your meaning clear at a glance.

Graphic Element: An image or graph supporting the key idea of the slide conveys far more than even the most exquisitely written prose on slides.

> ### *Images Trump Text*
>
> "When it comes to memory, researchers have known for more than 100 years that pictures and text follow very different rules. **Put simply, the more visual the input becomes, the more likely it is to be recognized – and recalled.** The phenomenon is so pervasive, it has been given its own name: the **pictorial superiority effect**, or **PSE**.
>
> "The inefficiency of text has received particular attention. One of the reasons text is less capable than pictures is that the brain sees words as lots of tiny pictures. . . .
>
> "Reading creates a bottleneck. My text chokes you, not because my text is not enough like pictures but because my text is too much like pictures. To our cortex, unnervingly, there is no such thing as words."
>
> John Medina
*Brain Rules: 12 Principles for Surviving
and Thriving at Work, Home, and School*

You can make your own master slides in PowerPoint to save formatting time and keep your slides looking polished. With only three elements in play, it's not as daunting as it might seem.

Illustrate, Don't Decorate

You can do your audience a huge favor if you use your slide to *illustrate* your point.

Now, this is not simply a matter of slapping some clip art on the screen to make it more interesting visually. Your images need to *communicate*, not just decorate. In fact, if you include images that are not clearly connected with the key message of your slide, you actively dilute your message, and retention by people in your audience will be even less than if you had simply hit them with a wall of text or bullet points.

Use your photos and other images *to help convey the key idea*. Got some numbers you want people to understand? Instead of organizing them in columns, try a pie chart or x-y axis or some other graph to help your audience understand the *meaning* behind your numbers.

Have a process or a sequence to share? How about a flowchart or a timeline or a map?

Or if using a table really is the most effective way to convey your meaning, try replacing words with symbols wherever possible. It's easier and faster for your audience to grasp "↑5%" & ↓400 units" than "5 percent increase" and "Down 400 units."

Another thing images do in a far more compelling way than words is to help make concepts more concrete. Your learners will relate better to an image labeled "11 football fields" than "3,960 feet." If you are teaching people how to allocate their assets as they near retirement, instead of just talking about different financial "buckets," try using an image of an actual bucket. Not only is that an analogy most audiences can relate to, but it also goes a long way toward making extremely abstract concepts more accessible.

Images can also add emotional punch to your message, which makes it more memorable. Your point about an aid program for tsunami victims will have more staying power with a picture of a devastated homeowner surveying the wreckage than mere numbers or graphs. Or use a photo and a short quote to humanize a story.

Before and After: What Happened Here?

We won't lie. It will take you a little longer to compose your individual slides if you follow these guidelines. But this consideration for your audience will help them absorb your meaning in far less time than they would if you limited your slides to the built-in templates. And it makes you more effective at the front of the room.

When you are laying out your slide to make the key idea easy to spot, just remember that images trump words, and concrete trumps abstract.

But Letters and Words are Images Too, Right?

The lines, curves and diagonals of each letter are processed by different parts of the visual cortex.

"The visual analysis we do has many steps. The retina assembles photons into little movie-like streams of information. The visual cortex processes these streams, some areas registering motion, others registering color, etc. Finally, we combine that information back together so we can see."

John Medina
Brain Rules: 12 Principles for Surviving and Thriving at Work, Home, and School

"The brain does not go straight from the images of words to their meaning. An entire series of mental and cerebral operations must occur before a word can be decoded. Our brain takes each string apart, then recomposes it into a hierarchy of letters, bigrams, syllables, and morphemes."

Stanislas Dehaene, *Reading in the Brain*

Less is more

Don't make your audience work to dig out the most relevant data for your point.

Only include relevant data on your slide

Your audience may not reach the same conclusion you did about the same data.

Don't make the audience do math
Show them what the numbers mean.

Don't make your audience read long narratives
For really long blocks of text, the words may be too small for your audience to see.

Don't read directly from your slides
The audience can read it a whole lot faster than you can say it. And if they can read the whole thing by themselves, why do they need to hear you?

Illustrate a story
The pictures add emotional punch, which makes it more memorable. This also reduces the temptation to read directly from your slide.

Group the things you want to compare
Don't make your audience keep jumping back and forth between two blocks of narrative, for example, or worse, between two slides.

For comparisons, find the common axis
This makes it easier to group similar things, and makes interpreting the slide a lot faster.

Replace words with universal symbols where possible
It is much quicker to grasp ⇧ than "went up."

What is the purpose of your list?
The revised slide communicates a growing global presence, as the headline and map make clear.

If you also wanted to illustrate the sequence or speed, you could communicate that idea by adding the location and name of each of the cities one after the other in a build.

New Locations in FY 2009

Six new locations were opened
- Los Angeles
- Buenos Aires
- London
- Frankfurt
- Tokyo
- Sydney

Target locations for 2014
- Singapore
- New York
- Paris
- Moscow
- Beijing

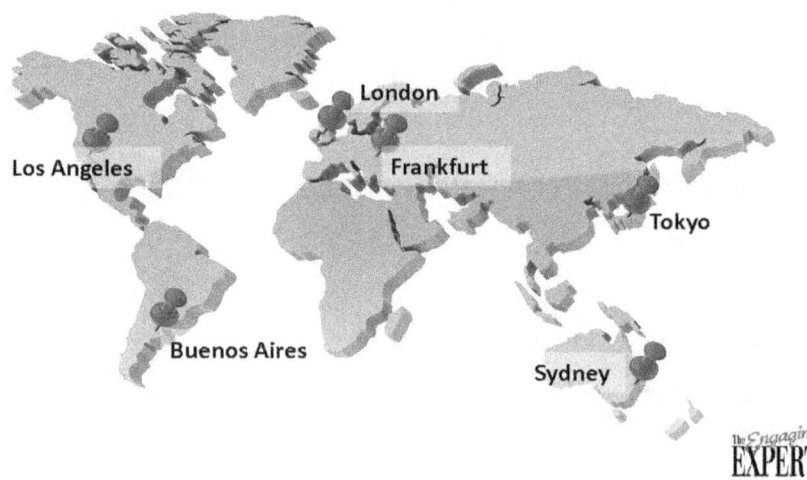

Make your title into a headline
Help your audience see the meaning they should derive from the slide right away.

Concrete trumps abstract
Look for analogies your audience can relate to.

Make sure critical facts and numbers are easy to see
Your audience does not have to dig for them in a block of text.

Strip all but the most essential text
You can give the comparison verbally here, since the point of the slide is to illustrate available choices of abstract things.

Adolescent Brain

- More gray matter than white matter
- Prefrontal cortex growing and developing
- Brain continues to grow and matures by the age of 25
- Teenage brain has a well-developed accelerator but only a partly developed break
- New proliferation of neurons at 11 for girls and 12 for boys

Photo humanizes the meaning
A bulleted list can't convey the same emotional punch.

Participant-Centered Handouts

With PowerPoint a near-mandatory element of many presentations, it is no surprise that handouts are so often merely copies of the slides.

It is alarmingly simple to do, of course – just a matter of clicks built into the program.

But what exactly are you trying to accomplish with your handouts? Do the preprogrammed options in PowerPoint serve the purpose you are trying to achieve?

Why Are You Using Handouts?

Do you want to . . .

- Reinforce your credibility and professionalism?

- Add supporting data, summaries, and reading lists?

- Reiterate your message?

- Engage your audience's participation?

- Help your audience remember your message?

- Give your audience a way to contact you in the future?

- Articulate a call to action?

For adventuresome souls like us who make their handouts from scratch, there seems to be two dominant schools of thought:

One is to design reference material that can be consulted whenever the need arises.

The other is that handouts should be working documents that engage the learner and make no sense to someone who was not present at the session.

Our own materials tend to do both. We include a "workbook" section intended to be used during the session for taking notes and doing structured activities. We want people to do a lot of writing and interacting with these pages, since it is one more way of engaging more parts of the brain and activating more "hooks" for learning to stick to.

Since lots of people tend to like reference materials (whether or not they ever look at them again after leaving the room), we also generally include a section explicitly labeled as reference. This is where we put our lists of additional resources, detailed appendices and related articles we want to share (with permission from the authors, of course).

However, to increase the likelihood of audience members actually using the reference section at some point, we make a point to refer to it often. We point out specific pages related to whatever we just covered, and sometimes we use narrative-heavy pages in that section for teach-backs and other in-class activities. The point is to be sure people have interacted with the material before they leave the room, because if they haven't, the odds of them ever looking at it drop precipitously.

When you design your handouts – if you use them at all – think through exactly what you are trying to accomplish with them. This will go a long way toward suggesting what non-PowerPoint-template form they should take.

Does It Belong in Their Heads or in Their Hands?

If you are helping pilots learn a new skill, one that involves making split-second decisions, it makes sense that whatever expertise you are sharing with them should be deeply internalized. They should be able to demonstrate and describe in detail what they know and how they would act on it in the specific conditions of applying that new skill.

But what if what you are teaching is an administrative task these pilots are only called on to do a few times a year? Are you better off making sure they know all the details of the procedure at the time they leave your session, or making sure they know how to use the tools and reference materials they will need to figure out the details at the time they are doing this infrequent task?

Or let's say you are teaching new employees to use a particular technology. The landmark discoveries that led to the development of your hospital's cutting-edge functional magnetic resonance indicators (fMRI) might be terribly significant or fascinating to you – and quite possibly to some of the people on the receiving end of orientation. Besides, it's perfectly logical to start at the chronological beginning of a story, right?

But how will it help the new lab techs do their jobs? Do you really have the time and resources to pad your training with the "nice to know" when they could be practicing a critical part of the process they are expected to execute? Besides, they can only absorb so much new material at once. Maybe that delicious bit of background information belongs in an appendix to your handouts for the people interested in that content to review at their leisure.

Here's one more example. Let's say you are an attorney specializing in land-use regulations for municipalities, and you have been asked to speak to a group of newly elected city officials from the region. How many times per year are they likely to need detailed answers on land-use questions, such as a request from a citizen group to hold a rock concert uptown or an application to build an additional parking lot for a thriving business? What resources will be available to them when they do need to address such questions?

With that in mind, which should you focus on in your presentation to make the best use of everyone's time?

- ❏ *Learn all the current regulations*
- ❏ *Learn and practice how to find answers whenever questions arise*

Here are some situations to help you sort out what to spend precious face-to-face time on from what could be handled with a job aid. They come from Allison Rossett and Lisa Schafer's book, *Job Aids and Performance Support: Moving From Knowledge in the Classroom to Knowledge Everywhere.*

Performance support (job aids) are appropriate . . .

- ❏ When performance is infrequent
- ❏ When the situation is complex
- ❏ When the consequence of errors is intolerable
- ❏ When performance depends on a large body of information
- ❏ When performance is dependent on knowledge or information that changes frequently
- ❏ When there is a high turnover rate
- ❏ When there is little time or money for training

And here are a few final tips about making your job aids into something your learners are likely to use back in the Real World.

Don't make it too detailed or too dense. That defeats the purpose of a job aid, which needs to be easy and quick to use.

Make its appearance distinctive. Most job aids end up staying forever in a file or tucked in the binder of handouts that accompanied training. Make yours stand out from the sea of 8½ x 11 white paper your participants inhabit. Use card stock, or laminate it, or make it an odd size or bright color. Make it easy for people to post in their cubicle or in their locker.

Have participants make their own. This has the advantages of helping your learners process your content more deeply *and* using a format they will like.

Preparation Checklist

With all the things on your mind as you get ready to deliver presentations or workshops, it's easy for some details to fall through the proverbial cracks. The humble checklist can make all the difference.

During Week Prior to Session
Create/assemble any visual aids or posters:
Confirm equipment needed:
Confirm location and equipment setup needs:
Create PPT—Load to laptop/save to flash drive
Copy Materials ❑ Participant handouts ❑ Materials for participant activities ❑ Job aids
Day of Event
Load PPT
Set up projector as needed
Arrange all supplies and handouts in the order in which they will be used
Stage visual aids, hang posters
Set participant tables (Sticky notes, blank paper, markers, name tents, etc.)
Set up resource table
Set up refreshments table

It's show time. You know how your session will benefit the organization. You know the key behaviors you want participants to practice, and you have devised ways to keep them deeply engaged. All your supporting materials are ready and looking terrific. You may even have practiced your intro, closing and transitions, or even the whole presentation. And now you are ready to take center stage.

Gulp.

Will your participants see you as the competent expert you are, ready to help them learn useful things?

As it turns out, picking up a few high-impact tricks of the presentation trade will not only showcase your expertise but also help your learners absorb your message.

WOW YOUR AUDIENCE!

Bad training is a monologue delivered in the presence of hostages.

—Sardek Love

I have never had anyone write in an evaluation that they wished there had been more lecture.

—Bob Pike

If you have applied any of the recommendations from the previous chapters about focusing and structuring your session, you are already light years ahead of what most audiences are expecting. Adding the finishing touches in the upcoming pages will knock their socks off.

Even if you have not had a chance to try out the content of the first four chapters, the ideas in this chapter will add polish and even pizzazz to any presentation.

This list is far from comprehensive, of course. We selected practices we have found to be most impactful in our combined experience of 58 years delivering presentations and training.

Environment Matters

First impressions set the tone for your session. After all the effort you put into preparing it, why start with a fizzle? Why put your participants through the awkward, fidgety silence that typically reigns until a critical mass of people arrive? And why launch your session with a tedious list of announcements or even a lengthy description of your credentials and how happy you are to be there?

A few simple techniques will not only make the quality of your session stand out, but they will also help make your participants ready to learn – and retain – what you are there to share.

Visuals

This does not simply mean decoration, although decoration is appealing, and it naturally provokes interest. Purposeful use of posters and other visuals associated with your content will provoke curiosity about what the visuals mean and how you will use them. Terri and Sheila often deliberately use posters with few or no words precisely to encourage speculation on the meaning of the model (like the Performance Impact Model, for example) or images. Think of it like baiting the hook for learning.

And as you are well aware, having visual reminders of key concepts stay in view for the entire session also reinforces the concepts, of course, and helps people remember them.

If you particularly want to draw attention to a specific poster or visual and get people talking, try putting it on the floor by the entrance. This is a clever place to put "ground rules," for example, or reminders to silence electronic devices. Over the refreshments table is another spot for these sorts of materials, since for many participants that will be their first stop when they arrive.

Music

It's hard to top the impact of music for setting the tone as people arrive. Want to prime people for an active session? Have high-energy music in the background as they arrive. Going for something serious and dignified? Go for classical music, especially baroque. Trying to encourage participants to interact with each other? Play something light and fun.

Be deliberate in your choice so you are setting the energy level where you want it right from the moment your learners walk in the room.

Ragged start

Give people something to start on – something relevant to *do* – as soon as they walk in the room. It should be something easy to work on alone or, better yet, in pairs or small groups. The directions should be simple and straightforward, requiring little if any explanation from you. Since a trickle of participants will be walking into the room right up until the official start of the session, you want your "ragged start" to be something people can join in whenever they happen to arrive.

This can be something simple like making a nametag. It would be better to provide a handout with instructions to introduce themselves to at least two other participants and jot down what they are hoping to learn in your session. (Note that this is still focused on your content, not something random or unrelated to the purpose of your presentation.)

Even better yet, get your audience to interact with your content immediately. Providing a relevant activity that can be done in pairs or small groups as people arrive accomplishes, at a minimum, two significant things.

First, it encourages participants to interact with each other right away. (Remember AIIM from chapter three?) This matters! Not only does it set the tone for interaction you have planned for the session, but also accelerates getting people comfortable and ready to learn. Among other things, pairs and small groups settle into productive work faster when they have already established even a tenuous relationship with others in the group.

Second, you are providing value from the moment your participants arrive. Giving them a chance to jump right into what they are there to learn is usually a pleasant surprise, and it establishes immediately that you are there to help them learn.

Here are a few tips to remember about using a ragged start:

1) Make it relevant but not essential. By definition, many of your learners will miss all or most of a ragged-start activity. Your intent is to provide additional value, not to penalize.

2) Make it something that calls for interacting with other participants. Individuals can request information from other individuals. Pairs or small groups can work on things together.

3) Make it something easy for people to begin with little direction from you, and easy for people to join in progress.

4) Be sure to "debrief" the activity after the formal start of your session. It does not have to be right away, particularly if you announce that you will be coming back to it later. But to help people retain what you were hoping to accomplish with the ragged-start activity, be sure to close the loop in some way.

Practice Before the Lesson

A project-management course began by asking arriving participants to find a partner and review projects described on posters around the room — the kinds of projects they would be participating in or leading after the training. For each sample project, the pairs identified the first two specific actions they would take to get the project started.

After the formal start of the session and introductions, the facilitator asked volunteers to share the actions they identified, which provided not just a launching point but also realistic context for introducing the "planning" phase of project management.

Walk in the Customer's Shoes

A customer-service course had vivid examples of excellent customer service posted on one side of the room and appalling customer service on the other. Arriving participants were asked to look them over while they waited for the session to begin. Shortly after the formal start of the session, the facilitator asked participants to describe the feelings evoked by the sample scenarios, and several people expressed surprise at the intensity of their own reactions. The emotional hook kicked off an increased level of interest from the very beginning of the workshop.

Match your layout to your purpose

If you have a chance to control how the space is arranged, take full advantage of the opportunity. What set-up will best suit what you are trying to accomplish with the number of people you have? How much interaction do you want to encourage? How much room do your learners need for the rehearsal opportunities you have planned? What about media that you'll want participants to focus on?

	Advantages	Disadvantages
Stadium Style	✓ Accommodates very large groups ✓ Good visibility to screen/charts	✓ Discourages interaction among participants ✓ Encourages learners to be passive ✓ Difficult for the facilitator to move around
Classroom Style	✓ Accommodates large groups ✓ Good visibility to screen/charts	✓ Limits interaction among participants ✓ Limits interaction of back participants with facilitator ✓ Difficult for facilitator to move around ✓ Too much like school

Chevron	✓ Good visibility to screen and charts, etc. ✓ Great for small group work ✓ Can accommodate large groups	✓ Limits large-group interaction ✓ Limited interaction of back participants with presenter
Basic U Shape	✓ Business like ✓ Good participant visibility ✓ Facilitator can walk in middle	✓ May be too formal ✓ More difficult for small-group work
Small Tables	✓ Informal ✓ Great for small-group work ✓ Great for group interaction ✓ Facilitator can assist small groups	✓ Some participants may have their backs to the facilitator ✓ More small-group "noise" ✓ May be too informal

Snacks and Learning

Your brain is acutely sensitive to glucose, the form of sugar that travels in your bloodstream. As the Franklin Institute explains, glucose is the only fuel normally used by brain cells. But unlike other cells in your body, neurons cannot store glucose, so they depend on the bloodstream to deliver a constant supply of this precious fuel.

> Too much sugar or refined carbohydrates at one time can actually deprive your brain of glucose – depleting its energy supply and compromising your brain's power to concentrate, remember, and learn. Mental activity requires a lot of energy.
>
> A sugary snack or soft drink that quickly raises your blood sugar level gives you a boost (and any caffeine adds to the lift), but it's short-lived. When you eat something with a high sugar content, your pancreas starts to secrete insulin. Insulin triggers cells throughout your body to pull the excess glucose out of your bloodstream and store it for later use.
>
> Soon, the glucose available to your brain has dropped. Neurons, unable to store glucose, experience an energy crisis

So if you are going to serve food or beverages at your session, you may want to include a high proportion of complex carbohydrates, which act somewhat like a time-release capsule for glucose. You don't have to get rid of the donuts, but consider supplementing them with fruits and vegetables, or breads and crackers made from whole grains.

If you are providing a lunch, try keeping it light, and favor salads and proteins over refined carbs.

The Care and Feeding of Learners

What is the single most important thing the brain requires to be able to learn?

A feeling of safety.

John Medina explains it this way:

> "The brain's primary interest is survival. That overshadows all other concerns. The brain is not interested in learning. The brain is interested in surviving. Every ability in our intellectual tool kit was engineered to escape extinction. Learning exists only to serve the requirements of this primal goal. It is a happy coincidence that our intellectual tools can do double duty in the classroom, conferring on us the ability to create spreadsheets and speak French. But that's not the brain's day job. And when the brain's safety concerns are not met, it will allow its neurons to moonlight during classes." (*Brain Rules for Baby*)

The more quickly you can establish a comfortable environment with a focus on what the participants are there to accomplish, the more quickly they will open up and start to learn.

Visit with Participants as they Arrive

When you are the facilitator, it pays to arrive early enough to spend time talking with participants as they arrive before your session starts.

And it's not only because you can pick up useful information about the group, like recent events or other tidbits you can work into your presentation. When you interact with individuals and small groups before your session starts, groups tend to open up noticeably faster.

Another seemingly little thing that packs a big impact is to learn and use participants' names. (It's okay to "cheat" by jotting down who is sitting where on a makeshift seating chart.)

Visiting with people and learning their names also helps to personalize your session. It's quite powerful when you can say things like, "Jason and I were just discussing the challenges you all face because of the limited resources budgeted for this project."

Don't skip introductions at the start of your session

Even if you are extremely pressed for time, or you are addressing a stadium-style lecture hall crammed with people, you can still help them meet their fellow learners. It can be as simple as saying, "Take two minutes to turn to a person you don't know well and introduce yourself. Then tell that person why you are here today." (Notice that you are still tying this activity to your content. Yep, we think that's really important.)

With smaller groups you can easily use introductions to gather more information about your audience. When individuals give their name, have them add something helpful to you, such as how long they have been in the field, how much experience they have with your topic, or in what kind of environment they will be using what you are there to teach.

Have too many people to do individual introductions? Have people introduce themselves at their table groups and share the relevant information there. Then as a large group have a limited number of volunteers briefly explain what they heard at their table.

Introductions can, of course, be a spectacular waste of time when they go on too long. You might be surprised at the number of people who will thank you for having a timer visible so participants can see the seconds ticking down to the end of their allotted minute or two.

A tactic to use with a large group introducing themselves to neighboring participants is to ask them to stand in their place when they have finished. Seeing others standing creates some pressure to finish.

Start with evaluations

You can accomplish several things by having your participants take a look at your evaluation sheet at the beginning of your session.

1) Encourage people to provide more thoughtful feedback throughout the session instead of in haste at the end.

2) Draw attention to what you are hoping to accomplish with your presentation.

3) Set your expectations of your learners.

Our own evaluations almost always include questions along these lines:

	Strongly Agree	Agree	Not Sure	Disagree	Strongly Disagree
I participated fully in the session.					
My co-participants were actively involved and supported my learning.					
If I were mandated to change one thing about today's session I would . . .					

They are effective reminders that, ultimately, participants bear responsibility for their own learning.

Participants also report that when they see the question about what one thing they would change about the seminar, they pay closer attention!

Invest their interest

A quick, simple exercise before launching into your content can help your learners absorb what you are teaching them. Prime them to listen for key ideas by encouraging them to think ahead to what is coming.

Preview the handouts: Invite your participants to scan their handouts for items of particular interest. You might say something like, "Take about three minutes to look through your participant materials, and highlight at least three words or phrases that particularly interest you or make you curious."

When time is up, ask for volunteers to share with the whole group what they chose to highlight. Now you have an opening to go in a number of different directions, such as,

- Make a brief comment on the items people name. ("That segment will build on what you learned last month about mixing cement in different weather conditions.")

- "Tease" what you have planned on the item, sort of like newscasters "tease" the stories they will cover in their upcoming broadcast. ("You put your finger on one of the most important concepts we're going to cover, John. We're going to do some intensive practice with that right after lunch.")

- Ask others who marked the same things to raise their hand so you can get a sense of what the priorities are of the people in the room that day. ("Did anyone else choose electroplating as one of their words or phrases?")

Speculate about visuals in the room: Invite volunteers to guess how you plan to use materials in the room or what the posters might mean. ("How do you think this contraption at the front of the room would be used in animal husbandry?" or "What do you think that chart on the wall has to do with the rules for municipal elections?")

List their expectations: Have a few volunteers share their top priorities for the session, and write them on a flipchart or white board. ("Sarah, what is the most important thing you want to learn today?" or "Jamal, what is it that made you choose this session over the others being offered right now?")

This gives you an opportunity to manage expectations that might be out of the scope of the session ("In today's session we will not be covering the tax implications of the ownership model you choose, but I can direct you to some excellent resources for that if you'll come see me during a break.") or to adjust your presentation to meet the priorities of the particular group. ("It looks like this group is especially interested in using social media in their marketing plan, so would you like me to focus more on that than on this other part of the agenda?")

All three of these techniques – previewing the handouts, speculating about visuals in the room, and listing expectations – actively engage your participants. And all three introduce an element of mystery of sorts. ("What *does* that graph in the handouts mean?" "How will this guy address my priority?")

Your learners will be listening to hear the answers to their questions, which engages more parts of their brains than just passive listening without a personally meaningful agenda.

(By the way, any of these could serve very effectively as an opener at the beginning of your session.)

Adapting for time or group size

What if it is more than a little impractical to solicit lots of responses from your group? You might find yourself running behind in your session and needing to limit the time for sharing. When a group is large, you can only hear from a small percentage of your participants.

But one of your priorities is to keep everyone engaged.

So instead of asking individuals to share with the large group as a whole, have people share with a neighbor or with their table group. Then, if you have time, ask for a few volunteers to share the most interesting thing they heard.

Help them think deeply about your topic

When you really want to help a concept stick with your learners, have them do some "deep processing" on it. Merely hearing it or reading it is generally not enough. Superficial processing of the sort called for in most multiple-choice or matching activities doesn't move the needle much either.

A simple, seemingly small change in approach, however, improves retention dramatically. Instead of asking participants to "read" a list, try asking them to "rank" the items on the list according to, say, what is most relevant for their particular circumstances. Or ask them to "evaluate" the list. Or have them pick out their top three favorites on the list.

None of these things are particularly hard for learners to do — or for presenters to work into their sessions. But each of these requires a higher level of thinking than simply trying to take in new information.

Using this approach can be a particularly effective CFU (Check For Understanding) and/or a way to close the loop on a segment of your content.

Here are some ideas to encourage learners to engage more of their brains in digesting what you are teaching:

- Rank or prioritize concepts

- Compare or evaluate concepts

- Put steps in the correct sequence

- Choose what is most important or relevant for them

- Identify their favorite(s)

- Describe how they feel about a given concept

- Describe or commit to a specific action the material suggests

- Generate arguments supporting or opposing the material

- Discuss a concept with a partner

Pop quiz! Which is right?

1. *Learners learn better if the response they emit is out loud or written down — an overt response.*

2. *Learners learn better if the response they emit is in their heads — a silent or covert response.*

3. *Learners learn better if they respond. There is no significant difference between overt or covert responding.*

Correct answer: 3. "What the research shows is that active responding is the critical ingredient. What is also important is that the response be a meaningful one.

Harold Stolovitch & Erica Keeps
Telling Ain't Training

Use Visuals to Convey your Content

Vision trumps all other senses. Of the total input coming into your brain from your five senses, approximately what percentage comes from each sense?

Sight: 83%
Hearing: 11%
Smell: 3.5%
Touch: 1.5%
Taste: 1%

Source:

Harold Stolovitch & Erica Keeps

Telling Ain't Training,

Not convinced? A famous wine-tasting experiment at the University of Bordeaux ("'ground zero" of the wine-tasting world) stunned even the researchers.

> What if we dropped odorless, tasteless red dye into white wines, then gave it to 54 wine-tasting professionals? With only the visual sense altered, how would the enologists now describe their wine? Would their delicate palates see through the ruse, or would their noses be fooled?
>
> The answer is "their noses would be fooled." When wine tasters encountered the altered whites, every one of them employed the vocabulary of the reds. The visual inputs seemed to trump their other highly trained senses. (John Medina, *Brain Rules*)

What does this mean for you when you are trying to help people learn about your area of expertise? The more you can use visuals to convey your message, the better.

Research shared by Stolovich and Keeps showed that you will get roughly three times better recall for visual information than oral. Combine simultaneous oral and visual combination, and you end up with roughly six times better recall. (Note: This conspicuously does *not* hold true when someone is reading aloud text that learners can read for themselves, of course.)

That's plenty of motivation to convey as much meaning as you can with images, graphs, and other visuals.

Movement for everyone

Unless you are using deliberate tactics to keep your participants engaged, their attention will begin to drift after about 10 to 20 minutes. By about 20 minutes blood has begun pooling in the lower part of the body. Movement sends a boost of oxygenated blood to the brain.

It doesn't have to be dramatic movement, and you can keep even this related to your content. (Yep. We still think that's really important.) Check out some of the energizers later in this chapter for ideas on making the content connection.

Movement in feedback

Terri and Sheila addressed a professional association that met in the evening, when members' energy was at a low ebb after a long day at work. Instead of doing a written CFU (Check For Understanding) at one point, we wrote out questions on flipchart paper, one question per page, and posted them around the room.

Participants wrote their responses on sticky notes and stuck them on the corresponding flipchart pages. Then they walked around the room to look at all the responses shared by their colleagues, which provoked interesting conversations to build on when the large group reassembled.

Never do for participants what participants can do for themselves

Adults, as you recall, like having choices and control in their learning. You can accommodate this *and* make your own job a bit easier.

For example, instead of you handing out materials, have designated participants get them from the front and hand them out to the group. Instead of you writing a group-generated list on the white board, have a volunteer do it.

This can also be a useful technique to minimize the disruption of any monopolizers in the room. If someone is dominating the discussion too much, give that person responsibilities that help the session go smoothly.

Minimizing Mayhem

One of the indicators of a facilitator's skill is how she or he manages key transitions from one type of activity to another, such as launching or ending small-group discussions, or selecting participants for particular roles. Here are some tips that will help you manage the learners you have worked so diligently to engage.

Getting the group's attention

The energy and engagement you get from having participants interact with each other in pairs or small groups is invaluable. Getting their attention back on you can be a frustrating exercise that leaves you looking ineffective. Techniques like the following work quickly and keep you in control.

- **Quiet Directions:** "Raise your hand and I'll know you are ready to move on." Keep repeating this at a normal volume, and as more and more hands go up, the volume will drop quickly.

- A large-group variation on this is to say in a normal voice, "If you can hear my voice, clap twice." Only a few people will have heard you, but their two claps will get the attention of more people, who will then catch on when you say, "If you can year my voice, clap five times." If the resulting claps do not bring quiet to the room, go one more round. "If you can hear my voice, clap four times."

- **Chime:** Use a chime, train whistle or other sound. You can improvise a "chime" using a glass of water and a pen.

- **Flash the Lights:** Flip the lights on and off like they do to signal the end of intermission at a play or concert.

- **Use Music as Cue:** Start music to signal the beginning of a group activity. About 30 seconds before you want them to stop, start turning the volume up gradually so they can't help but become aware of it. Then stop the music abruptly. People will realize something has changed and will wrap up their conversations.

Cut Discussions a Little Bit ...

... short. Yes, you read that right. Deliberately stop small-group and pair discussions slightly before people are finished talking.

Russian psychologist Bluma Zeigarnik observed that people remember uncompleted or interrupted tasks better than completed ones. She theorized that interrupted activities create "psychic tension" in us that acts as a motivator to drive us toward completing the task or finishing the business. It's called the Zeigarnik Effect.

> For facilitators this means stopping small-group discussions when you notice the volume in the room is just starting to drop after reaching its loudest. Then "finish" the idea as a large group.

Establishing groups

You can squander an awful lot of time having participants group themselves. Speed it up, make it genuinely random, and add an element of the unexpected by using categories like these.

- "If your **birthday** is in the first half of the year, go to this side of the room; if your birthday is in the second half of the year, go to that side of the room."

    You can also divide groups by which quarter of the year their birthday falls in, or even which month to get lots of groups. You will probably need to adjust the group sizes after the fact with these options, but it's plenty easy to do.

- "If you **listened to the radio** on your way here this morning, raise your hand. You are the _____ group."

- "If you **eat your corn on the cob** side-to-side, go here; if you eat your corn on the cob around the ear, go there."

- "Look at the **amount of green**, yellow and/or black you are wearing. If you have more green than the other colors, go to this corner of the room; if you are wearing more yellow than the other colors, go to that corner of the room . . . ."

- "Who is your **favorite James Bond**? If you prefer Sean Connery in the role . . . Roger Moore . . ." etc.

- "Everyone **choose a [candy bar]** from the pile on your table." (Wait for everyone to select an item from a pre-defined variety.) "All the people who chose [Milky Way], gather over here. [Salted Nut Rolls] gather over there . . .," etc.

- "Stand up and **find a partner from another table**, then share the answers you chose to the _____." (Allow time for partners to find each other and share.) "Now repeat that with a different partner."

- "Find a partner from a different part of the room who is **wearing the same color** you are."

- "Find the person in the room whose card goes with yours." (You will have already **randomly distributed cards** that "go together" in some way, e.g., bread/butter.)

- "Look at the **playing card** you drew when you came into the room. Form a group with the people who are holding the same suit as you are."

Choosing individuals for specific roles

Often in small-group activities you need someone to serve as the leader or table spokesperson or as the recorder taking notes or writing answers.

Randomizing how you choose an individual within a small group relieves some anxiety, often induces laughter, and maintains interest. Here are a few ways to identify specific people quickly and efficiently, with a dollop of humor that adds interest.

"Find the person in your group . . .

- whose birthday falls closest to today."
- who is the tallest."
- who is wearing the most red."
- with the most change in his or her pocket or purse."
- with the biggest face . . . on their watch!"
- who traveled the greatest distance to get here today."
- who most recently fed a pet."
- who has the most siblings."
- who has the most anatomical legs in their home."
- who most recently bought a book."
- who most recently delivered a presentation of some kind."
- who has done [your topic] before."

Tip: To add humor and an element of surprise, once you identify a specific person in a small group, indicate that the leader will be the person to his or her left, for example, or someone else in the group that the person you identified chooses.

Raising or lowering the energy in the room

To raise the energy in a quiet group,

- If you don't get any answers when you ask the large group a question, say, "Take 30 seconds at your tables and brainstorm the answer."

- Do a pairs activity. Having lots of people talking at the same time raises the level of energy in a room.

- Use high-energy music to set the tone during breaks and to cue the beginning and end of group activities.

- Introduce movement. For example, ask participants to answer a poll question by standing or moving to one side of the room or the other to "cast their vote."

To reduce the energy of a boisterous group,

- Do a small-groups activity using groups of at least 4-8. Having fewer people talking at the same time lowers the energy in a room.

- Do an individual reading or writing activity – possibly with calm music to cue the beginning and end of the time for individuals to work.

- Suggest a short break, during which you might put on soothing music.

Sprinkle energizers throughout your session

Lots of people roll their eyes at the prospect of "energizers" – and with good reason. Adults in a professional context expect to be treated like adults, and they don't want their time wasted on activities that have no clear bearing on the subject matter at hand.

Of course, given a choice, most adults would rather not be forced to sit for hours on end. As we noted earlier, after about 20 minutes or so, blood starts to pool noticeably in the lower extremities. Movement of any kind, however, sends a rush of oxygenated blood to the brain.

The trick is to make the movement relevant. Here are a few ideas for doing that.

- **True for You:** Have participants stand at their seats. As they hear each statement they should sit down and immediately stand back up again if the statement is true for them. (If it's not true for them, they simply remain standing.) It's important to start from and return to a standing position; that's what makes it such a powerful energizer. Statements you use are limited only by your imagination. For example,

    o Just for fun: "You remember exactly where you were when you heard Michael Jackson had died."

    o Learning about the group: "Your organization represents 50 or more unionized employees." Or "You have been in this industry for less than three years."

    o Reinforcing content: "You will have a chance to apply the _____ technique within a week."

    o Clarifying support: "Your organization has already begun using the _____ process."

- **Line-Up:** Have participants form a single-file line representing a continuum. For example, line up from most to least experience with your topic, or their degree of preference for receiving frequent feedback or being left alone unless there's an issue. You could even use birthdays in chronological order. There will be a great deal of discussion and milling about, but encourage the group to line up quickly rather than perfectly.

- **Human Bar Graph:** Put signs representing answers or preferences along a wall from left to right. Have participants go stand by the sign with their own answer. For example, "How frequently do you have to recertify your people at your workplace? (every year, every two years, every five years, only once)" or "How do you prefer to receive updates? (by email, by phone, in person)." If you have multiple questions, particularly if they aren't related closely enough to use the same set of answers, you can use letters or numbers instead. It's best to limit the number of options in that case to three or, at most, four.

- **Slow Count Self-Assessment:** Have participants rate their comfort level with a series of topics on a scale of 1-10. As you count slowly from 1-10, have them stand when they hear the number they gave themselves.

- **Chair Swap:** Use the same kinds of questions as in "True for You," but have participants seated in a circle. When they hear a statement that is true for them, they must find a different seat than the one they started in. (Yes, it's a variation on Fruit-Basket Upset that you played as a kid.)

Sometimes, like when the room is too warm or participants just finished lunch, you just need an energizer for the sake of an energizer. Here are two that can be done very quickly and still be effective.

- **Touch 3 Walls:** Yep, it's just as simple as it sounds. Have participants stand up, touch any three walls in the room, and return to their seats. You will be surprised at the impact on the energy and attention of the group – especially late in the afternoon. (You can also use this occasion to get participants to affirm each other's *active* participation by suggesting they use eye contact and shake hands with someone new on their way back to their seats.)

- **30-second stretch:** This is another one intended simply to wake up participants using movement. Just have them stand and stretch in their places. It can be helpful to have a PowerPoint slide showing 3-4 stretching exercises.

"In a moment ...."

When you announce that you are going to have your participants do something in pairs or groups, the immediate buzz of conversation tends to drown out your actual instructions.

Try starting your directions with a phrase like, *"In a moment* I'm going to ask you to find a partner from another part of the room." Or, *"When I give you the signal* to start, I'd like you to get in groups of three."

Then give your directions, which should include a mention of how you will end the activity and bring the group back together. Ask if anyone needs clarifications, and *then* say, "Now you can form your groups and start."

Don't waste a co-facilitator

Co-facilitators can support each other by keeping an eye on the energy, interest and potential confusion of participants when not at the front of the room, and bringing it to the attention of the current presenter.

We recommend having a couple of pre-arranged signals for things like calling for a break, indicating that the session is ahead of schedule or behind, and conveying that you would like to make a comment – particularly if you have not presented with your co-facilitator before.

Another way to help the person at the front of the room without interrupting or making someone lose face is to indicate you want to ask a question. When acknowledged, offer a comment like, "This is a particularly complex process. Would anyone like Ken to repeat the steps?"

Your co-presenters can also assist in other ways when not in front of the group. They can manage music or lights, help latecomers get caught up without disrupting the large group, collect written responses or votes from participants, or analyze responses.

Troubleshooting and improvising

No matter how carefully you prepare, you can't anticipate all the things that could mess up your plans.

The thing to remember when something goes wrong is, in most cases, your participants are rooting for you, and they can be your allies. They will reflect back at you whatever attitude you convey. If you appear anxious, they will get anxious. If you remain calm and cheerful, chances are they will too. And they are almost always happy to help you if you ask.

> ### Converting Reluctant Cops
>
> A group of police officers was less than enthusiastic about participating in mandatory Respectful Workplace training. Their body language and comments were unambiguous to even the inattentive observer. Rather than brace for combat, the presenter ditched her planned opener and asked instead for participants to share what they already knew about the topic. "Maybe I can eliminate some of these slides," she said.

> The comment was met with wild applause, and the attitude in the room shifted from sullen confrontation to cooperation around identifying the minimum amount of content necessary to fill in the gaps of what the group already knew.

> ### Fire!
>
> *Sheila relates the following incident from a training session for city employees.*
>
> I had arrived plenty early because I like to greet people as they arrive rather than still be scrambling to prepare the room. I checked the equipment, posted numerous visuals, calmed my jitters with music and began visiting with participants while they completed a ragged start activity.
>
> As I began to introduce myself, a layer of smoke began descending from the ceiling in the area where the projector was mounted. Many of us noticed but disregarded it until it got larger and thicker, at which point the fire captain (one of the participants that day) directed us to leave the room.
>
> I asked participants to help me gather up materials from tables and walls. It was a pleasant surprise that *all* the participants pitched in, even the street-maintenance workers who had made it clear they were not happy to be there in the first place. They picked up whole tables of materials

and moved them to another room that one of the participants quickly procured for us.

The smoke turned out to be a fire in the ceiling above the projector. (Thankfully, the projector was saved, though.)

The incident reminded me, though, that learners *want* to contribute, love being asked, being involved, and even the resisters should get the opportunity to be involved.

Too Much of a Good Thing

The first time Terri and Sheila presented together at a conference, it was at a break-out session, one of several that competed with some continuing-education (CE) options. We were hoping for at least 20 participants, and we created contingency plans for smaller numbers. We also make handouts for 40 just in case we got more people than we expected.

It was a shock but a pleasant surprise when closer to 100 people crowded into our space. Participants were gracious as we cheerfully modified our plans on the fly. Pairs activities became small-group activities. Large-group movement around the room became team projects. And handouts became reference materials for people sharing them and writing their notes on notebook paper. We offered to send copies after the conference to everyone who left a business card, which created an opportunity to collect additional feedback and to reinforce key content.

> The session was not entirely free of grumbling, of course. But when they were invited to help create the solution to the problem, participants were astonishingly cooperative and helpful. What could have been a miserable session ended up getting such good evaluations that conference organizers approached us about returning the following year.

The Polished Presenter

Here are a few additional tips to add polish to your "platform" skills. Most of these are things that few of your learners will be consciously aware of, but the impact can be substantial.

Minimizing jitters

Even the most experienced facilitators get the jitters. Really! So if you are a bit nervous before facilitating a learning event, that makes you exactly . . . normal.

A few habits will help you keep those jitters manageable.

Day(s) or Hours Before Your Session

- **Practice.** Yes, it seems obvious. And given your expertise with your topic, it probably seems unnecessary. But it's hard to overstate how much practicing your presentation – *out loud* – improves your confidence and polish. Speaking the words out loud exposes flaws that reading does not.

In an ideal world you get to practice the entire thing. More likely your world is less than ideal, so *practice the transitions between topics*. You'll be surprised at how much that helps you feel prepared. Rehearsing even one time will improve your confidence in your material.

- Do some **participant reconnaissance**. If you don't know the people who will be in your session, Linked-In can be a beautiful thing.

Right Before Your Session

- Take slow, **deep breaths**.

- **Stay hydrated** with water or a clear soda.

- Remember to **eat**! It's not always amusing when your stomach growls loudly at an inopportune moment in your presentation.

- **Stage your materials** (handouts, props, etc.) in the order in which you will use them.

- **Arrive earlier** than you think is necessary. This gives you time to set up the room and check your equipment before participants arrive. And it gives you "float" to accommodate unexpected delays, which is very good for your frame of mind.

- Take time to **greet participants** and interact with them as they arrive.

During Your Session

- **Let participants help** whenever possible. Remember the axiom from earlier in the chapter: "Never do for participants what participants can do for themselves." Have designated people distribute handouts, record on the white board, monitor temperature, greet latecomers, etc.

- Don't be afraid to **refer questions back to the group**. It may feel like that's cheating, but as long as you avoid looking panicked, it can actually make you look rather smart, and what expert doesn't savor that?

- **Use small groups** and partner discussions. Stepping out of the spotlight is actually helpful to your learners, and it takes the pressure off you.

After Your Session

- When your session is sandwiched between others, **enlist help** to collect your materials so that you aren't rushed right out.

- **Be available** for comments and questions. You might well hear something like, "This workshop was sensational! I learned more than I expected! When will you be back to address us again?"

- Reward yourself with a big glass of your favorite adult beverage!

Avoid this cardinal sin of presentations

Over and over again surveys about audience pet peeves show the same thing at the top of the list: **Don't read aloud blocks of text that participants can read for themselves.**

There's a good reason most audiences react negatively to this. Our brain can process visual input a whole lot faster than auditory input; so your participants can't help but read ahead. Then what they are seeing and what they are hearing are out of sync. The inputs are literally competing with each other. Guess what happens to retention then?

Hold their gaze

As you speak, make eye contact with *individuals* in different parts of the room.

Try to hold a person's gaze for about 3-5 seconds. Less than three often makes it look like your gaze is shifty. Five seconds can seem like an eternity to you, but it's not likely to seem so long to the other person. Go much more than five seconds on average and you will both start to feel a little weird.

Make a point of meeting the eyes of people in the corners and sides of the room. Without deliberate intention to do otherwise, it's easy to stay focused on the middle and make the people around the periphery feel a bit left out.

Fade to black

You know better than to compete with your slides for your audience's attention. Slides are there to *support* you in communicating your message.

Many speakers are good about covering the projector or turning it off or using a blank slide when they don't need a slide showing. An easier, less obtrusive way to turn "off" your PowerPoint temporarily is to insert black slides at certain points in your presentation. Not only is the black slide faster than manually adjusting the projector and less jarring than a white screen, it can serve as a reminder to you as the facilitator that it's time to move on to an activity or a break.

Move away from the soft speaker

Is someone answering your question too softly for you to hear what they are saying?

Don't move toward the person. This gives the speaker no reason to speak louder.

Get answers from everyone

Sometimes you get better results by having participants talk to a partner or small group.

Large-Group Discussion	Small groups/partners
• Speaking up can feel risky for individuals.	• Shy people have an easier time sharing with a partner or small group.
• Few participants are active at the same time.	• All participants can be active at the same time.
• The shy people won't share in front of the whole group.	• Changing from large group to partner to triad to large group provides variety in your pacing.
• Makes it easy for monopolizers to monopolize.	

Show that you really want a response

Three small changes in how you ask for questions can make a really big difference.

1) Banish the usual formulation, "Do you have any questions?" For one thing, asking a yes-or-no question does not encourage discussion. Instead, say something along the lines of, "What may I clarify?" or "Who wants to open with the first question?"

2) Give people time to reflect. Asking a question and not giving people time to develop a response suggests you are not really interested in the response anyway, so why bother to answer? If you are tempted to fill in the silence, take a drink of water while you give participants time to think.

3) If no questions are forthcoming, have one ready for them, such as, "What other consequences will there be for the change in the

regulation?" or "What comes to mind when you think about implementing this with your team?"

Prime the pump

When you ask a question of the large group, and you give learners time to formulate a response, sometimes you still get . . . crickets. Rather than let the awkward silence drag on, say something along the lines of, "Take 15 seconds and tell a partner how you would answer that question." Once people have had a chance to do this, you are much more likely to get a response when you re-pose your question to the large group.

When you want the large group to generate a *list* of some kind, prime the proverbial pump by providing the first few items yourself. This helps focus participants and gives them momentum rather than starting from a dead stop.

You can also get many more contributions to your list when you give them 15 seconds or so to jot down three or four items themselves first. Then have them share what they wrote with a small group.

To minimize the risk of speaking up in shy groups, ask participants to share something they heard from their partner or group without identifying whether the idea was their own or someone else's.

Manage large-group questions

- Make a habit of repeating questions from your audience to make sure everyone has heard them. (This also buys you a bit of time to formulate your response.)
- Other ways to buy time:
    o Ask the person to repeat the question.

- o Say, "Let me make sure I understand your question. You're asking me . . . ."

- o Ask the person what he or she thinks would be an appropriate response.

- o Take a sip of water.

- o Pause. It's okay to show that you are reflecting on your answer.

- Maintain eye contact with the person while he or she is posing the question. Then scan the room to include everyone in your response. You can put a figurative bow on top by returning to the questioner with, "Does that answer your question?"

- Neutralize a negative question. Respond to "Why are your services so expensive?" with "Your question has to do with how we structure our fees . . . ."

- Don't bluff if you don't know the answer. You can actually turn this into a credibility asset rather than a liability. For one thing, audiences appreciate the authenticity. For another, you can demonstrate your professionalism by offering to find the response and share it within a stated period of time.

Manage your time

Start your session exactly on time. You never want to punish the people who arrived on time by making them wait for the people who didn't.

You can use peer pressure to help participants return from breaks on time. For example, promise small prizes to the table groups or rows that are all in their seats when it is time to start up again.

You can also assign a person at each table or each row to ensure that all the people in that group are back in their seats on time. Consider offering rewards for the people-wranglers who are successful in this effort

Tweak your agenda

Avoid printing specific times on participant agendas. Participants can become nervous if they see you are significantly off on timing, and they don't have any way of knowing, for example, that you are covering something originally planned for later or that you can shorten an upcoming activity.

You can also make things easier on yourself by printing your own (detailed) copy of the agenda on brightly colored paper so you can spot it easily amid handouts and other papers.

Pencil things in ahead of time

Nervous about your ability to write or draw neatly on a flipchart in front of an audience? An easy "cheat" is one you can do ahead of time: Lightly pencil in the letters or images you want to draw. Then you simply trace over them with a marker when you are in front of the group.

On a related note, consider asking for a volunteer to draw for you. Surprisingly, "experts" emerge from the crowd most of the time.

You did it! Your session was a great success, and the "smile sheet" evaluations your participants turned in reflect not only the fact that they think you are a swell facilitator, but also that they believe they will be able to transfer what you taught them into the messy, often chaotic reality of their everyday lives. Score! Affecting their performance in the Real World was, after all, your objective.

Did it work?

Thanks to the questions you asked when you were first approached to share your expertise, you can demonstrate that it did.

MEASURE YOUR IMPACT

"Evaluating 'training' instead of performance is akin to evaluating the wedding instead of the marriage."

—Robert Brinkerhoff

"I enjoyed it." "I can perform on the job."

—Cathy Moore

At this point it is perfectly understandable if you indulge in a tiny bit of feeling smug. Most presenters, including an astonishing number of people who earn their living as professional trainers, get to this point and say, "Oh, yeah. We had better do some sort of evaluation. People expect it."

You, on the other hand, have this already covered for the most part, since you took the time up front to identify exactly what you were trying to accomplish and how you would measure it.

Assessing the impact of classroom learning in a workplace or professional setting is not an exact science, of course. Most of the time there are far too many other factors affecting performance to point to an exact cause-and-effect result.

But because of your efforts early in the process, you are well positioned to show a powerful correlation that is relevant to the organization.

Why Are You Collecting Feedback on Your Session?

Not all reasons are created equal. Being mindful of what you are gathering for what purpose will go a long way toward determining how much time and energy you should devote to evaluating your session.

- ❏ Meet expectations of sponsors who expect evaluation forms after every training
- ❏ Provide participants a means of giving feedback
- ❏ Provide feedback to participants needing a passing score on a certification exam
- ❏ Collect cumulative data on which you, the facilitator, are evaluated
- ❏ Identify areas of improvement in content, materials and presentation
- ❏ Justify resources allocated to providing the session
- ❏ Demonstrate a need for additional resources (training, presentation, job aids, etc.)
- ❏ Gather insights on how participants will apply what they learned
- ❏ Determine what follow-up to provide after the session
- ❏ Gather testimonials for future presentations
- ❏ Affirm that you, as facilitator, hit the mark!

What Is Your Purpose in Evaluation Anyway?

What information you collect depends on who will be using it and why. The feedback you need as a facilitator is necessarily different from the needs of, say, senior management or the sponsoring organization. If no one (including you) is going to use the data you collect, then you are probably better off not collecting it in the first place. Why waste the time and resources of all the people involved? (Besides, if no one is going to use the data you collect, you risk alienating those who expect that their input will make a difference.)

What Do These People Want from Evaluations?	
Presenters/Trainers 	• Did participants like it? • How polished was my delivery? • Was it organized well? • Were the rehearsal opportunities relevant and effective? • Will participants be able to apply what they learned?
Participants 	• Can I communicate what I did or did not like? • Can I communicate what I found most or least useful? • Can I communicate how I think the session could be improved?

Supervisors	• Will the performance of my direct reports be improved? • Is there follow-up I need to provide? • Was it worth it to have my people sitting in a classroom instead of doing their work?
Senior Management	• How did it serve IRACIS? (Increase Revenue, Avoid Costs, Improve Service) • How will it help the organization meet our goals this year? • Was training worth the time, expense and other resources we dedicated to it, or would they be better budgeted somewhere else?
Sponsoring Organization	• How well do participants understand the vision of the organization and how their work affects it? • What issues surfaced that might affect the whole organization?

Senior management, by the way, is probably not terribly concerned about whether your participants had a good time, liked the food or thought the presenter was exceptionally charming. "Smile-sheet style" evaluations generally have little of real interest to this level. Even if leadership is keeping track of hours of training delivered or the number of "butts in seats," these tend to be peripheral issues (at best!) to their concerns about the overall functioning of the organization.

The moral of the story? Figure out who will want or need the data you collect and the conclusions you draw from it. You probably did most of this already back when you were approached to deliver a session in the first place, back in chapter one. Your efforts to target measurable results from the get-go will make you stand out.

Kirkpatrick's Levels of Evaluation

No book about workplace learning would be complete without at least a brief explanation of Kirkpatrick's levels of evaluation.

Donald Kirkpatrick is considered the godfather of training evaluation. While there are other well-known models out there, his seminal work first published in 1959 established the now-classic levels of evaluation, typically depicted as a pyramid.

You might notice that the categories correspond rather well with the types of feedback of interest to the range of people above.

If you were to Google it, you find a staggering amount of recent material debating the merits of the Kirkpatrick model and its variations. Among workplace-learning professionals it's quite trendy at the moment to publish passionate defenses or reinventions or even outright rejections of the original levels of evaluation.

The important point for occasional presenters and accidental trainers is to be able to show value beyond the reactions typically collected in "smile sheets." And since you started *developing* your presentation with an eye on the top of the pyramid, you will have a far, far easier time demonstrating value than most people, who put together an evaluation after the fact simply because that is what people expect.

Including Evaluation in an Initial Proposal

The language of the proposals frequently used by Terri and Sheila include explicit references to Kirkpatrick's levels of evaluation. Below is an excerpt from an actual proposal.

Measures of Success

Level 1 Evaluation: Reaction – *Did They Like It?*

> We provide a comprehensive survey identifying participant-satisfaction ratings on facilitation, materials, logistics and engagement. Participants also identify at least one area for improvement after each session; these inform how facilitators adapt subsequent sessions to the needs of the particular audience. All sessions include frequent opportunities for participant feedback.

Level 2 Evaluation: Learning – *Did They Learn It?*

> Multiple *checks for understanding* (CFUs) are sprinkled throughout each session to ensure understanding of concepts and key messages. While these take many forms, the most important is probably the "rehearsal opportunities" in which participants practice applying their new learning the way they will use it in the real world of their work.

Level 3 Evaluation: Application – *Can They Apply It?*

> Each participant will develop and share an Action Plan describing the specific steps they commit to

> taking as a result of what they learned in the session. Optional follow-up includes surveys based on these Action Plans (sent three months after the training) and brief interviews of selected participants' leaders.
>
> **Level 4 Evaluation: Impact** – *What Was the Impact?*
>
> Randomly selected performance evaluations will be reviewed to evaluate documented professional development goals. A follow-up summary and recommendations will be presented to a designated sponsor representing [the company] after the data from the three-month survey and interviews is compiled.

Baseline Comparisons: Your Most Powerful Tool

Ideal, of course, is to use some metric that the organization is already in the habit of tracking. Sales, for example, are typically documented with great care and detail. So finding before-and-after numbers is relatively straightforward.

You may recall the list of possible measures back in the first chapter, *Begin With the End in Mind*. Many of those items are already tracked, so you would not have to generate new data.

What happens when you need to measure something that has not been tracked before?

Sometimes you will be fortunate enough to get your sponsor's help in collecting new information that can be used as a baseline. More often than not, other people need to be involved too, such as supervisors or clerical staff. If you read the medical call center example on page ___, you may be freshly aware of the wisdom of including some of your target audience in establishing what your session is intended to accomplish.

Involving other people in collecting baseline and comparison data is ideal, since it aligns the agendas of the people affected, and it builds ownership of the results.

Sometimes, however, you need to set your own baseline. For that you can use tools like a pre- and post-session test, pre- or post-session surveys, for example.

These do not have to be elaborate. It could be as simple as asking your audience to rank their current proficiency with your topic at the beginning of your session and returning to the question at the end.

Tests Can Be Used to Teach

Many certification programs culminate in one or more tests, often measuring both declarative knowledge (What do you know? What can you explain?) and procedural knowledge (Can you perform the target skills?).

Don't forget that a well-designed test can be a teaching tool, particularly when you accompany it with detailed corrective feedback. As you recall from chapter 3 Prepare to Engage, the more your learners practice actively recalling from memory what they need to know and (more importantly) *do*, the better they learn it. Practice tests added to, or in lieu of, review sessions will produce much more powerful results than review alone.

Do You Even Need a Written Test?

If your learners can demonstrate to you that they can perform in a realistic rehearsal situation, you have probably established that they know what you need them to know. If the context does not mandate a written test (e.g., company policy or government requirements), it may be that you don't need one at all.

Qualitative Data Counts Too

When people talk about qualitative questions in evaluation, more often than not they are referring to questions that encourage some sort of free-form response. It can be hard to summarize and measure this kind of data.

But you can find ways to measure most things. If you need to share open-ended responses concisely, a useful tactic is to establish categories for the answers you get.

Some you can identify in advance. For example, if your evaluation or other feedback mechanism asks, "How did you learn about this session?" you can usually anticipate the communication channels involved. (Supervisor? Company intranet? Colleague?)

Other categories may take you by surprise; you might see a pattern in the responses you get that you wouldn't have guessed in advance. ("Look at that! Almost a third of the participants said that their most useful insight came from that activity with the potato!")

The qualitative responses you collect will probably be of most interest to you as the facilitator. (Especially when you get to read/hear things like, "The presenter was totally awesome!") But it can be quite powerful for the people with whom you share your data.

You can use qualitative data not only to demonstrate that you met the objectives you identified before you started, but also to help you show the meaning behind the numbers.

You can call out generalities, like the percentage of participants who believe participating in your session will have a "noticeable" or "very noticeable" impact on their performance, for example. Or you could pull actual quotes typifying a type of response and indicate the number of people expressing a similar idea. The level of detail you use will depend, of course, on your purpose in compiling the information in the first place and on your target audience reviewing your results.

For mission-critical initiatives of the organization, it might be worth doing some serious digging to assess your results. If it's big enough, you could even go so far as to use focus groups and interviews days or weeks after your session. The impact of a lunch-and-learn, on the other hand, might be adequately assessed with a show of hands to answer questions before everybody gets back to work.

Before and After your Session

Just because you didn't get to collect baseline information before your session starts does not mean that you can't assess before-and-after states. Ask participants to self-report the change. For example, at the end of your presentation, ask participants to rate what their level of anxiety about a pending merger probably was before they walked in the room and at what it is right now.

Sample Questions for "Smile Sheet" Evaluations

There are volumes written about evaluation forms and best practices related to them. We will limit our recommendations on this topic and instead provide some samples that you might find useful in choosing what you include in the evaluations you create.

Our principal advice is that you include both quantitative and qualitative questions in your smile sheets. Having questions that only require a checkmark or a number or letter as a response – essentially multiple choice – makes it easy and fast for participants to complete your form. It's easy to quantify and aggregate these answers. And sponsors tend to like reports with actual numbers. If you craft your questions to focus assessing on your target outcome, you can get useful, meaningful data from these sorts of evaluations.

You probably won't want to include too many open-ended questions. Even if you only have one or two, most people will not provide detailed responses. *But* the people who have strong opinions – positive or negative – about some aspect of your session will often give you very useful feedback. A handful of these more than compensates for the vague, abbreviated responses that the majority will provide.

Do they KNOW it, or Can they USE it?

It's easy and tempting to write activities that test whether learners **know** something. How can we make learners **use** their knowledge as well? [. . .]

- **Know** activities ask learners to retrieve and maybe categorize or explain information.

- **Use** activities ask learners to apply information to realistic situations.

Often, a "use" activity includes a test of whether the learner "knows" something — you get two activities in one!

USE It!

Your learners create widgets. To speak with their coworkers, they need to know some technical terms. One term is "transmogrification," which means modifying a widget so it will work at high altitudes. What can we do to help learners master this term and the related concept?

Know activity: Drag the term to its definition — drag "transmogrify" to "modify a widget so it will function at high altitudes."

Use activity:

"Your client wants to use their widget at 2800 meters above sea level. What modification do you need to make to the widget?"

- Transmogrify it
- Redorbinate it
- Neoplyordinize it
- No modification needed

The "use" activity tests whether the learner can apply their knowledge of transmogrification **in a realistic situation**, not in an abstract definition activity. At the same time, it answers three "know" questions for us. It tells us whether the learner knows that:

> 2800 meters is officially "high altitude"
> You need to modify widgets for high altitudes
> The necessary modification is called "transmogrification"

> Of course, if these bits of information are crucial or frequently misunderstood, we'll want to have more questions or activities to reinforce them. Also, our feedback goes beyond "correct" or "incorrect" to show the consequences of the learner's choice and reinforce stuff some more.
>
> If you write strong "use" activities, you don't need to write "know" fact checks at all.
>
> Cathy Moore, Instructional Design Consultant
http://blog.cathy-moore.com
reprinted with permission

Our other piece of advice you already saw in chapter four: Include questions about participants' own level of involvement and that of their fellow learners during the session. When you point this out at the beginning of your session, it usually has a noticeable impact on the level of ownership participants demonstrate.

Besides, pointing out the evaluation at the beginning and asking people to fill it in as the session goes along usually results in more thoughtful responses, particularly if you remind people about it once or twice well before the end.

Odd- or Even-Numbered Scales?

Some people are quite passionately committed to their position regarding whether to allow a "neutral" response in multiple-choice evaluation questions.

Should your scale look like this?

Strongly Disagree	Disagree	**Neither**	Agree	Strongly Agree
1	2	3	4	5

Or like this?

Strongly Disagree	Disagree	Agree	Strongly Agree
1	2	3	4

Is it a cop-out for participants to give a non-committal, neutral response? Or is a lukewarm answer a useful bit of data?

We simply suggest that you take care to be consistent and unambiguous about whether the positive and negative options run from left to right or right to left. One early draft of an evaluation form we wrote had two different, conflicting scales on it, which would have caused some head-scratching by users. (Don't worry. We caught it in time.)

Below are a few questions to help you craft your own "smile-sheet" evaluations. You wouldn't use all of them in the same evaluation, of course; you'd pick out two or three that will get you the best information for your purpose in collecting the feedback in the first place.

- I have changed my views about _____

- I have improved my ability to _____

- I have learned _____

- I have learned new ways to _____

- I have learned better ways to _____

- I now know the appropriate procedure to _____

- I still have a question about _____

- I'd like more information on _____

- A great follow up to this session would be _____

Sample Survey from The Engaging Expert Workshop

Session Date _____

Facilitator(s) _____

Content	Strongly Agree	Agree	Not Sure	Disagree	Strongly Disagree
I learned or re-learned information and skills I can apply in the *Real World*.					
I received what was promised.					
The content was neither too advanced nor too basic.					
The materials were effective in helping get the information across.					
I had opportunities to practice and get feedback on the skills I was learning.					
I found value in the resource materials.					
Facilitator(s)	Strongly Agree	Agree	Not Sure	Disagree	Strongly Disagree
Demonstrated knowledge of the content.					
Presented material in a clear, organized way.					
Modeled the information being taught.					
Used a variety of methods that helped me learn.					
Showed interest in participants.					
Answered my questions thoughtfully.					
Participants and Environment	Strongly Agree	Agree	Not Sure	Disagree	Strongly Disagree
I participated fully in the session.					
My co-participants were actively involved and supported my learning.					
The location and quality of the site was appropriate.					
Overall Satisfaction	Strongly Agree	Agree	Not Sure	Disagree	Strongly Disagree
I achieved my learning goals.					
What I learned will help me or my business/department/team meet our goals.					
Overall I was satisfied with the session.					
I would recommend this session to others.					
Additional Comments					
The best, most useful part of this session was . . .					
If I were mandated to change one thing it would be . . .					
Other comments:					

Other Simple Ways of Collecting Feedback During Your Session

Plus/Delta (+): Participants jot down one or multiple things that went well or that they liked about the session under the "+" sign, and one or multiple things that participants didn't like or recommend changing (Delta is a symbol for change in chemistry and other disciplines) under the "" sign.

Most/Least Useful: Change up the focus of the +/ question by asking participants to identify the single most useful and least useful aspects of the session.

Aware/Avoid/Act: Name something you became *aware* of during the session that will affect how you operate at work; name something you will *avoid* as a result of what you learned today; name a specific way you will *act* on what you learned today – with someone who participated in the workshop and with someone who did not attend.

When Your Audience Is Too Nice

Sometimes people are reluctant to "hurt your feelings" by sharing useful critiques. Written or verbal, their feedback on how to improve your session next time around tends to be bland at best.

One way to protect both the participant's sensibilities and your ego as a presenter is to phrase the question in terms of, *"If you were mandated to change one thing,* what would it be?"

Ask-It Basket: This is a simple way for participants to provide anonymous feedback, which shy groups and individuals may value. Point out either a physical basket or a designated flipchart page in the back of the room at the beginning of your session. Ask participants to pose questions or request clarification by putting a question in the ask-it basket (or a sticky note on the flipchart page), which you will check periodically throughout the session.

To make effective use of this technique, consider doing the following:

- Provide slips of paper or sticky notes and something to write with right next to the ask-it basket. Make it spectacularly convenient to use.

- Put the ask-it basket in a high-traffic area, such as near the door or the refreshments.

- Remind participants at least once, and preferably more often, that you are actively monitoring the ask-it basket, looking for their feedback. It can be easy for people to forget – including you!

- Ask a volunteer to monitor the ask-it basket. Often they will add to it themselves if no one else does. They may also encourage others to post a question.

- Ask everyone in the group to write a question for the ask-it basket.

Post Your Questions: If you have a small number of feedback questions you want participants to answer, consider writing one question each on pieces of flipchart paper you can post around the room. Arm everyone with sticky notes or/and something to write with, and have them circulate to post their answers by each question. (See example on page ____.) In addition to providing safely anonymous feedback, this one serves as an energizer by getting people moving.

True for You (see page 169): Just adapt your statements to reflect what you are trying to evaluate. For example, "The pace of this session was a bit too fast for me. . . . too slow for me . . . just right for me." If you use this technique, be mindful of peer pressure. Seeing how a majority of the other people respond will affect participants' answers.

Human Bar Graph (see page 169): This is a handy way to show ratings on a scale. You could put four or five pieces of paper on the wall or on the floor with the numbers 1, 2, 3, etc., and ask participants to line up in front of the number that reflects their response. For example, "On a scale of 1-5, how valuable was this session to you in your work?" Here again peer pressure will affect responses.

Rating with Your Fingers: Instead of physically moving to stand by a number, participants can remain seated and show their number with their fingers while you scan the room to get a general sense of the group's response. (If you plan ahead you could even have numbered cards on hand for participants to use for this purpose. They are easier to see than fingers.)

Spur-of-the-Moment Evaluations

Most of the above examples could be improvised at the end of your session if necessary. (They could also be part of a "smile sheet" evaluation form, of course.) For any of the examples, you could ask participants to share their responses in one of several spur-of-the moment variations, such as:

- Writing their responses on a piece of their own paper
- Writing their responses on sticky notes, one answer per note
- Posting sticky-note responses on designated flip charts
- Posting sticky-note responses on designated walls
- Doing any of the above in pairs or small groups
- Doing any of the above verbally in small groups that report to the larger group

- Writing on a flipchart or white board answers provided verbally by volunteers in the large group

Words and Actions

> When she had a rather large audience, Sheila asked them to get into groups of six to eight and gave them instructions to share two things with their group:
>
> 1. One word or phrase that best describes your learning experience today ("I told them I wouldn't accept ho-hum words like 'good' or 'great' or even 'excellent' – and of course *not* 'lousy' without explanation.")
>
> 2. One specific action you will take in the next two weeks.
>
> "Then I modeled what I was after by saying, 'I'm *energized* by the great ideas I heard today, and within the next two weeks I will incorporate your suggestions into the recommendations in my report.'"

Unexpected Lemonade from Behavioral Lemons

Sheila relates a time when she was dreading the evaluations but she did them anyway.

I was feeling pretty low about the feedback I anticipated at the end of day one of a two-day session. Some very difficult behaviors during the session, including loud talking from small groups and several interruptions with laughter, distracted the other participants and me.

After they finished writing their action plans, I had people gather in a circle at the back of the room, and I provided two questions:

1. On a scale of 1 to 5, with 1 being low and 5 being high, how would you rate the value of this session to your job? Why?

2. How could you have improved the value of this session yourself?

While several participants gave the session a 4 or 5, there were predictably some low scores from people who specifically identified the distractions as the problem.

What surprised me was that these same people admitted that they had the power to ask their fellow participants to quiet down, and that this would have improved their experience. Interestingly, the next day the difficult behaviors did not arise.

WHAT WILL *YOU* DO?

"Boring experiences that make people suffer aren't going to change anyone's behavior."

—Cathy Moore

"Learning in today's companies is much like teaching someone to ride a bike. At the end of the day, the question isn't what resources you provided but rather whether they can perform the task at hand."

—Michael E. Echols

Teaching other people about your area of expertise probably isn't your regular job. But the seemingly little change in your approach to how you do that – starting with what you want your learners to *do* after they leave – vaults you ahead of most other presenters. There are plenty of professionals in training, public speaking and teaching who never think through this question.

So what now? What will *you* do back in your Real World with the tools you found in this book?

Just like the people you teach, you will need to practice. In your case it may well be in front of a live audience when you deliver your next presentation. That's okay. Even fairly small changes in the direction you have chosen can have a significant positive impact for your learners and for the organizations that invite you to share your expertise.

Just like the people you teach, you will need to break down the larger chunks of things that are mostly new to you, then gradually combine them and add layers of nuance over time.

Your first attempt to link your efforts to IRACIS might feel rather contrived and draw blank stares from your sponsor. But it will still make your session better than if you hadn't asked those questions in the first place.

Trying to isolate key behaviors and imagine ways to mimic their context in the conference room or lecture hall may not come naturally to you. But the experience you provide your learners will be richer for it.

Some of the more dramatic departures from the familiarity of lecture could be too far outside your comfort zone for now, and your next deck of slides or packet of handouts might not look as different from your prior efforts as you thought they should. But you will have given your materials more "hooks" for your learners to grab and retain.

Initially you will probably use only a handful at best of the delivery tips that happen to be new to you. The effect will still be gratifying – especially if your audience doesn't even notice the smooth implementation of things that used to be awkward or time consuming.

After your session you might discover that you hadn't identified quite the right metric in those initial planning conversations to be able to measure the specific improvement you were after. But you have fundamentally altered your approach to helping others learn – altered it for the better.

And that's what you wanted in the first place, wasn't it? You have deep experience and hard-earned expertise that other people recognize. They want to benefit from it, and you want to share it. When you take the time to enable others to apply *your* gifts in *their* settings, the Real World is a better, richer place for all of us.

ABOUT THIS EDITION'S PRIMARY AUTHOR

Sheila Krejci, M.Ed. HRD is a performance consultant inspiring business owners, corporate leaders at all levels and professionals in many industries to design and deliver compelling presentations with a call to action for their audiences. Her vision, to help "experts" get what's in their heads into the performance of their audiences, inspires workshops like *Intentional Speaking©*, *The Accidental Trainer©* and *The Engaging Expert©*.

Integrating foundational adult learning theory with practical application is the hallmark of Sheila's engaging style with audiences nationally. Author of Networking is a Lifetime Skill and co author of The Engaging Expert: a Fieldbook for Occasional Presenters and Accidental Trainers, Sheila has been an adjunct staff member of the University of Minnesota, the University of St. Thomas and the Minnesota Partners in Education in Minnesota.

An award winning facilitator of Inscape Publishing's DiSC and Everything DiSC professional development tools, Sheila frequently speaks using "alternatives to lecture" at national conferences of ASTD, SHRM, ISPI and Training 2012 at the Georgia World Congress in Atlanta.

 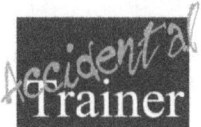

HELP ME HELP OTHERS

As a life long learner inspiring life long learning, I'm interested in your 'tools, techniques and examples' that I can share with future *Engaging Expert* audiences. Please send your contributions along with your name and contact information to

                Sheila@sheilaktraining.com.

If your ideas are incorporated into the next version of this Fieldbook, we'll credit you as a contributing author!

www.ingramcontent.com/pod-product-compliance
Lightning Source LLC
Chambersburg PA
CBHW032251150426
43195CB00008BA/414